TRUE CRIME KILLERS

VOLUME 1

Ben Oakley

SELECT TITLES BY BEN OAKLEY

FICTION

HARRISON LAKE INVESTIGATIONS
The Camden Killer
The Limehouse Hotel
Monster of the Algarve

HONEYSUCKLE GOODWILLIES
The Mystery of Grimlow Forest
The Mystery of Crowstones Island

SUBNET SF TRILOGY
Unknown Origin
Alien Network
Final Contact

NONFICTION

TRUE CRIME
Bizarre True Crime Series
Monsters of True Crime Series
True Crime Killers Series
Orrible British True Crime Series
The Monstrous Book of Serial Killers
Year of the Serial Killer

OTHER NONFICTION
The Immortal Hour: The True Story of Netta Fornario
Suicide Prevention Handbook

As a thank you for adding this book to your collection, we would like to offer you a FREE eBook for simply signing up to our mailing list. Along with a free book, you'll get weekly updates from the world of true crime brought to you by truecrimelists.com, and early book release notifications so you can be the first to get them at an introductory price, exclusively for subscribers.

Visit WWW.TRUECRIMELISTS.COM and click on FREE BOOK from the menu.

Copyright © 2023 Ben Oakley.

First published in 2023 by Twelvetrees Camden.

This edition 2023.

The right of Ben Oakley to be identified as the Author of the Work has been asserted by him in accordance with the Copyright, Designs and Patents Act 1988.

Visit the author's website at www.writetheplanet.co.uk

All rights reserved. No part of this book may be reproduced, or stored in a retrieval system, or transmitted in any form or by any means, electronic, mechanical, photocopying, recording, or otherwise, without express written permission of the publisher.

Each case has been fully researched and fact-checked to bring you the best stories possible and all information is correct at the time of publication. This book is meant for entertainment and informational purposes only.

While the publisher and author have used their best efforts in preparing this book, they make no representations or warranties with respect to the accuracy or completeness of the contents of this book. Neither the publisher nor the author shall be liable for any loss of profit or any other commercial damages, including but not limited to special, incidental, consequential, personal, or other damages.

The author or publisher cannot be held responsible for any errors or misinterpretation of the facts detailed within. The book is not intended to hurt or defame individuals or companies involved.

ISBN: 978-1-915929-10-5

Cover design by Ben Oakley. Images by Marina Luisa.

For information about special discounts available for bulk purchases, sales promotions, book signings, trade shows, and distribution, contact hello@twelvetreescamden.co.uk

Twelvetrees Camden Ltd
71-75 Shelton Street, Covent Garden
London, WC2H 9JQ

www.twelvetreescamden.co.uk

True Crime Killers Volume 1

The Telford Necro Monster 19

DeFeo: The Real Amityville Horror 29

Smelly Bobby Tulip 43

One Infamous Murder & Seven Suspects 53

The Wedding Day Murders... 71

He Chose To Kill on Saturday Nights 81

The Slave Master Killer.. 91

Blood & Fire At Christmas 103

Killer in the Navy 113

The Scream Killers 125

Bow Cinema Axeman 135

Horror Movie Killer 145

Satanic Murder in a Church 155

A Twist in the Murder Tale... 163

The House of Blood Murders 173

Black Mass Poisoner 183

Killer In the Walls.. 195

The Ughill Hall Murders.. 203

18 real-life stories of serial killers and murderers with solved and unsolved killings from the USA, UK, Europe, and beyond.

A note from the author.

Thank you very much for choosing this book for your collection! The true crime community is one I've fallen in love with over the years and I'm truly grateful for your support. To readers new and old, I raise my glass to you. In fact, it's down to my readers that this new series exists at all.

The mission behind TRUE CRIME KILLERS is as simple as it sounds, to share with you stories of real-life murders and the killers behind them. The cases are laid out in a concise, easy to read format, with all the facts and information you need. If you want a 300-page read on each case, this is not that book.

This is a true crime anthology series with 18 stories in each volume. Inside each volume you'll discover serial killers and murderers with solved and unsolved killings from the USA, UK, Europe, and beyond. Some you know, some you don't.

Many of the other series' released through Twelvetrees Camden are general true crime anthology books. They include the whole gamut, from murders to robberies and frauds to cybercrime. But TRUE CRIME KILLERS has one focus – murder.

Which needless to say means some of the stories contain descriptions of such an act. Where other books go all in on the gore, there is some restraint shown here – as much as is possible. But this is not a book about fluffy rabbits, it's a book about humans killing other humans, so expect a little darkness to come your way.

Just remember that true crime addiction is not a curse, it's an outlet. Along with other authors in the true crime genre, we know that you have a desire to be fed your prescribed dose of true crime and we are all more than willing to satisfy the hunger.

Why? Because we live and breathe true crime stories everyday of our lives. We surround ourselves with research material at the detriment of our own downtime, picking and choosing what should go in to make the story flow – to meet the needs of our readers.

I suppose it's another way of saying that true crime writers are here to serve you – the reader. Without you we are nothing at all. So, here's to the true crime community, young and old, and a promise that we'll always keep you up in the middle of the night.

Now I've rambled long enough, I hope you're still here! Grab your drink of choice, kick back wherever you are and let's enter this fluffy rabbit hole of darkness together.

Ben Oakley, Jan 2023.

Introduction.

There is perhaps nothing more intriguing and yet horrific than the thought of one human killing another but it is more common that we want to believe. When we're safe at home, wrapped up in warm clothing with our loved ones nearby, we like to believe the world is a happy place, overrun with peace, joy, and the good things in life. We come to believe in the righteousness of humanity.

Except, not all humans are good creations.

Killers hide among us and they're not always in the shadows. That neighbour down the street you've never spoken to might be harbouring a terrifying secret, a body under the patio, a victim in the basement. The person behind you in the supermarket queue or sat next to you on the train could have already claimed a life and are seeking out the next notch on their belt.

Serial killers, mass murderers, killers of children, monsters in the darkness, they all exist alongside us. They move among us in secret hoping not to be caught, wary of the cameras and passing police. They lay in wait for the next victim, stalk us and herd us into their world, imagining how they might end our lives. When our veil of safety gives way to comfort and we let our guard down, that's when they strike.

Humans killing humans is not a modern evil, we have been killing each other since the dawn of humanity. Even the bible proves we are split between the dark and the light. And yet it is the darkness that tempts those to push a knife into flesh, shoot a bullet to the head or choke the life out of one they once loved.

Simple logic suggests there are active serial killers out there in the wild, preying on unsuspecting victims and evading capture. For each serial killer who has ever tarnished history, there have been thousands of murderers. They are single-kill criminals who lashed out in a moment of anger, revenge, or lust, premeditated or not.

Murder is the ultimate sin – the taking of another's life. It is the removal of a person from the human race forever. Most murderers and serial killers are caught before long, held to account for their crimes and judged in the courts of justice. But there are those who commit the sin and for whatever reason get away with their crimes.

For those who escape the long arm of the law, they might be judged in the afterlife as they approach the pearly gates only to be sent to Hell. Despite the differences in body count, serial killers and single-kill murderers differ in many ways. There are said to be only fourteen reasons why serial killers kill, but they are not exclusive to one other.

Access to victims (victim selection). The toxic legacy of war. Abuse suffered in childhood. Influence of violent pornography. Cheap travel and open borders. Attitudes towards females (formed in childhood or via porn). Modern wave of disconnected living. Psychological damage caused by abuse or trauma. Impulsion to commit violence. Population increase (more potential victims). Hunger for fame or infamy. Desensitisation to violence caused by various outlets. Modern destruction of family values. Societal decline (unemployment, lack of police funding, fear).

Of course, they are not the only reasons why serial killers kill but they form the basis of an overall theory that postulates they are moulded by society, environment, upbringing, and way of life. They contribute to the ever-increasing opportunities afforded to those of a violent mind-set and enable them to act out on desires that may have remained dormant.

The same, however, could be said for single-kill murderers. The real reason anyone kills another human being is because of a situation they find themselves in or an opportunistic kill. What leads them to murder is incredibly individual to that killer and cannot always be generalised.

Which brings us nicely onto the varied stories of killers in this book. We traverse through the history of the known world from the UK to the USA and find a porn-obsessed sexual deviant, killer in the Navy, serial-killing truck driver, the true story of a haunted house, a killer who only killed on Saturday nights, and a whole raft of twisted tales.

First, a warning.

Due to the nature of this book and the subject it discusses, there are depictions of murder included in some of the stories. **This is from the outset of this book.** If you know what you are getting yourself into and know what real-life killers likely do, then let us proceed.

Here are previews of the 18 real-life true crime stories within these blackened pages.

The Telford Necro Monster

A porn-obsessed sexual deviant, with the potential to become a serial killer, became the youngest person to receive a whole life tariff, after killing a teenage girl and engaging in necrophilia.

DeFeo: The Real Amityville Horror

A haunted house, a violent history, an investigation by Ed and Lorraine Warren, dozens of movies, and the truth behind one of Long Island's most infamous family massacres.

Smelly Bobby Tulip

Robert Black was convicted of four murders but has been linked to at least 21 more, making him one of Britain's most prolific serial killers, with an unusual and disturbing taste for young girls.

One Infamous Murder & Seven Suspects

One infamous murder, seven suspects, infinite theories. You are dared to tread through a real-life horror story that has haunted and taunted investigators for quarter-of-a-century.

The Wedding Day Murders

While he was on the run from the law, a notorious criminal murdered three members of the same family, kickstarting a 39-day manhunt.

He Chose To Kill on Saturday Nights

A Welsh serial killer who raped and killed three girls in Port Talbot in 1973 on Saturday nights, was caught 30 years later – after his death – in the first case in history solved using familial DNA testing.

The Slave Master Killer

By day he was a Sunday School teacher and director of a charity, loved by his community, by night he was the slave master, the first internet serial killer who enslaved and butchered at least six victims.

Blood & Fire At Christmas

For survivors of the Covina Massacre, Christmas memories are now filled with blood and fire, and a loss of innocence ripped away by a man dressed as Santa, whose suit melted onto his own skin.

Killer in the Navy

A gay Petty Officer in the Royal Navy killed at least two young sailors and has since been suspected of killing up to twenty, in one of Hampshire's worst cases of serial killing.

The Scream Killers

Inspired by the movie 'Scream', two teenagers hide out in their friend's basement, to scare and kill their victim – while making their own macabre documentary about it.

Bow Cinema Axeman

During the Golden Age of movies, a cinema attendant took an axe to his manager and eloped with a suitcase full of money, in a tale of premeditated murder, historical horrors, and a fake death.

Horror Movie Killer

A man inspired by horror movies went on a rampage that left four dead and two injured, in a tragic case that laid the blame at the feet of those put in place to protect the public.

Satanic Murder in a Church

A young newlywed went to church to pray and fell victim to an evil killer who did unspeakable things to her body. The killer got away with it for almost half a century until he was finally revealed.

A Twist in the Murder Tale

After a body of a woman was found near a motorway, police rushed to her home to find her husband bound and gagged, claiming they were attacked by a man in a clown mask – but a twist this way comes.

The House of Blood Murders

An argument between lovers resulted in a triple murder at a house in Glasgow, branded the House of Blood killings, with the ringleader known as the mother of all evil.

Black Mass Poisoner

Black magic, witchcraft, poisonings, French aristocracy, hundreds of deaths, and a secret network of abortionists and fortune tellers, welcome to the tale of Catherine Monvoisin.

Killer In the Walls

A creepy intruder terrorised a family by living in the walls of their home and making them think the house was haunted, in a true urban legend that ended with multiple murder.

The Ughill Hall Murders

In a double murder that shocked Sheffield, a successful solicitor killed his mistress and her daughter, and left her son for dead, before fleeing to France and threatening to jump off the Amiens Cathedral.

The Telford Necro Monster

A porn-obsessed sexual deviant, with the potential to become a serial killer, became the youngest person to receive a whole life tariff, after killing a teenage girl and engaging in necrophilia.

The grim tale of 22-year-old Jamie Reynolds and his teenage victim, 17-year-old Georgia Williams, is as horrific as it was preventable. For many years, Reynolds had run-ins with the police for his behaviour against women but was allowed to continue to live in society as a free man.

This freedom allowed him to develop an obsession with dark pornography, to such a degree that he began doctoring BDSM images with the faces of people he knew. Born in 1991, Reynolds was born in and raised in Wellington in Telford, Shropshire, to hard working parents in a semi-detached house.

He left school with average grades and got a job working in a local shop but something had already begun to eat away at his mind and he couldn't ignore it. Reynolds had discovered internet porn by the time he was a teenager, and it caused an obsession that would ultimately lead to murder, with one psychiatrist fearing he had the potential to become a serial killer.

The seeds for the murder Reynolds would ultimately enact were laid during his teenage years. In 2008, when he was 17, he lured another 17-year-old female to his parents' home to pose in photographs for a fake media project.

When she refused to go to the upstairs room, Reynolds attacked her and attempted to strangle her. Fortunately, the unnamed female fought him off and was able to escape the house to call the police. Reynolds was arrested but claimed to have no memory of the attack.

The female had severe red marks and swelling around her neck, and had Reynolds sustained the attack then she would have been killed. Police found thousands of photographs on his computer that showed various unidentified females being strangled or suffocated. In two of the photos,

Reynolds had digitally added a noose around their necks.

He deflected police attention by claiming he had a pornography problem but said he would never look at such images again and reiterated that he had no memory of the attack. A simple apology later, and Reynolds was freed with no charges – only a warning.

Sexual deviant

When the murder of Georgia happened five years later, the public and researchers looked back on this incident as the moment Reynolds should have been stopped. Not only did this incident enrage those who read about the murder, it was literally attempted murder and brushed off with a warning.

But the signs didn't stop there. In 2011, when he was 20, he attempted to have sexual relations with a work colleague. When she refused his advances, he deliberately reversed into her car at high speed. She spoke to police about the way he acted around her before and after the incident, but this too was brushed off as an accident or misunderstanding.

By that time, Reynolds' interest in pornography had taken an even darker turn. He began writing stories featuring the names of females he knew.

They generally followed the same plot, in that he would lure them to his home or a remote location, photograph them, then strangle them and do horrific sexual things to their corpses.

In February 2013, three months before Georgia's murder, Reynolds lured another young female to his family home, while his parents were away for a two-week holiday. Two days prior, he had manipulated a Facebook profile photo of the girl to include a digital noose around her neck.

The young female arrived at his home and he locked the doors. He attempted to kiss and touch her but she refused his advances and she began screaming at him. An hour later, realising she would be heard, he helped to 'find' the keys.

Unknown to the girl at the time, Reynolds had planned to hang her in the attic of the home using a makeshift contraption he had been building. A note was later discovered reminding himself to remove the bar from the loft door and take the cable ties out of the drawer, ready to use.

Disturbing photos

When the planned murder fell through, Reynolds focused on the next window of opportunity he had. His parents were taking their next holiday at the end of May 2013, and he chose May 26th as the day when he would be able to claim his victim.

He began writing a story about 17-year-old RAF Cadet Georgia, which he titled *Georgia Williams in Surprise*, and finished three weeks before the date of the murder. He had become fascinated with her due to her red hair, which he had always taking a liking to.

Georgia was a well-liked young woman, who was a college mentor, student councillor, and head girl at school. She was planning to have a career in the RAF and was using the RAF Cadets as a stepping-stone to her dream.

In the story, Reynolds described her hanging from the rope. He wrote, '*I can't wait to see you dance for me. I like my girls dead. That was a quality show babe.*' At around the same time, he messaged 16 other local young women he knew through Facebook and other social media, to see who wanted to come to the house.

Even in the messages, he stated that it would be for a photoshoot involving simulated hanging, which the women could use for a modelling career, and he for his photography aspirations. He messaged these women in case Georgia didn't take the bait.

Two of the women showed interest until Georgia agreed to the shoot, lured by his promise of photographs for use in the future. Realising his story was about to become reality, he purchased the clothes he wanted her to wear and the rope he wanted to hang her with.

On 26th May 2013, Georgia left her home under the premise of helping a friend improve his photography skills. She entered Reynold's home and never left alive. In the attic, Reynold's had placed an oar across the attic beams, where he had planned to hang Georgia.

She willingly agreed to stand on a box and have the noose placed around her neck. To continue the façade, Reynolds took some photographs of her with his stepfather's camera, for his personal use later on.

Before Georgia became suspicious of Reynolds true intentions, he moved behind her, kicked the box out, and pulled on the rope with all his strength. Georgia was dead within minutes. The photos of her before – and after – her death, were shared in court, and make for some of the most disturbing content this researcher has ever seen.

Necrophilia

After she was dead, he stripped her, took her body to his parents bed and took photos of himself having sex with her corpse, photos which lasted the course of an hour. He then took her to other rooms in the house and photographed himself in various sexual positions with the body.

After half a day of copulating with the corpse, he put a pre-meditated plan into action to cover his tracks. He used Georgia's phone to text her mother to say that she had left Reynold's home and was going to stay at another friend's house for the night.

At the same time, he cancelled the arrangements he had with the two other females who had taken an interest, saying that he would be elsewhere that night. When darkness set in, he put the body in his stepfather's van, along with her clothes, and drove to a remote area of North Wales. He also transferred the photos onto a memory stick and took it with him.

He even went as far as putting camping equipment in the van, as a cover story for travelling to Wales. While there, he left her nude body in the open, and buried her clothes and jewellery, which have never been found. Fortunately for the investigation, his van got stuck in mud close to the location he had left the body. Photos were taken of the van in the mud by the people who helped him get it out.

To continue the façade, he drove to Glasgow the next day and purchased some shopping items using his credit card to add to his story. But back in Telford, the police were already onto him. After Georgia's parents reported her as missing, Reynolds became the prime suspect.

He was arrested in Glasgow when the van and his credit card were tracked. At the time of his arrest, Georgia's body had not been found but police were informed of the pictures of the van in the mud. A day later, Georgia's decomposing body was found.

Life tariff

The investigation had all the evidence they needed, including the photos Reynolds had taken of Georgia before and after her death. Police discovered almost 17,000 images of extreme pornography on his computer's hard drive, along with almost 100 videos.

Almost all the files showed unidentified women in various BDSM poses, with most having a focus on strangulation, asphyxiation, and suffocation. There were also photos of local schoolgirls from Telford where he had digitally added a noose around their necks and handcuffs hanging off their wrists or ankles.

There were also 40 stories he had written, detailing exactly the horrific things he wanted to do to women, including hanging them. Many of the stories had the names of real females from the local community.

Fortunately, for Georgia's family, who were suffering immeasurable grief, Reynolds pleaded guilty to her murder, and a trial was avoided. Professor Peckitt, a leading psychiatrist, concluded his report by saying that Reynolds would be a danger to women for the rest of his life.

He also strongly believed that if Reynolds got away with Georgia's murder, that she would have been the first in a long line of victims. There was no doubt in his mind that Reynolds was a serial killer in the making.

On 19th December 2013, the judge handed down a sentence of a whole life tariff, making Reynolds one of a handful of criminals to have received the order. It meant that Reynolds was sentenced to life without the possibility of parole. It is the highest sentence anyone in Britain can receive.

An inquiry was raised almost immediately into the failings of police and social workers who knew about Reynolds behaviour since 2008. Within two years of the sentencing, 12 police officers were handed misconduct notices in relation to the case.

Reynolds was sent to Wakefield Prison, dubbed Monster Mansion, to serve out the rest of his life.

Though Georgia's murder could have been prevented, there is hope that the case will stop other such incident's from ever happening, meaning that Georgia's death may not have been in vain after all.

DeFeo: The Real Amityville Horror

A haunted house, a violent history, an investigation by Ed and Lorraine Warren, dozens of movies, and the truth behind one of Long Island's most infamous family massacres.

In 1977, American author Jay Anson wrote a book called *The Amityville Horror: A True Story*. He based the book on the real-life experiences of George and Kathleen Lutz, who claimed to have been terrorised by paranormal happenings at their house in Amityville, Long Island, New York, in 1975.

The book was made into an independent horror film in 1979, simply titled *The Amityville Horror*. It was the largest independent film of the time, grossing almost $90million at the box office and becoming the second largest film of the year behind *Kramer vs. Kramer*.

Then, as the sequels began to drop, something unusual began to happen. From 2016, small independent horror films began adding 'Amityville' to their titles to capitalise on the brand recognition, but many had no connection to the original book or film.

At the time of writing, there have been 42 films released based on the story of Amityville and using the original title as a stepping-on point. Those include 10 official sequels and a raft of VOD (video-on-demand) titles, including *Amityville in the Hood*, *Amityville in Space*, and – *Amityville Vibrator!*

In 2021 alone, there were six Amityville films released on an unsuspecting public. Despite the paranormal experiences of the Lutz family being the basis of the films, the true story behind the Amityville Horror is far less sensational but still haunts the town to this day.

Only one truth remained

Before the Lutz family made Amityville famous for all the wrong reasons, in 1974, Ronald DeFeo Jr. shot and killed his entire family as they slept in their beds. The location; 112 Ocean Avenue, Amityville, Long Island, New York, the same house where the Lutz family later experienced the horrors.

Just as the movies have confused the original story of the Amityville Horror, so too did Ronald, who changed his story over the murders multiple times. First, someone had broken into the house and killed everyone, then it was a mafia hitman, voices in his head, and his sister who he killed in a struggle.

Whatever version of the story came out, only one truth remained. In the early hours of 13th November 1974, 23-year-old Ronald awoke from his sleep, grabbed his .35 calibre rifle, walked through the house and opened fire.

He shot dead his parents, Ronald DeFeo Sr., 43, and Louise DeFeo, 43, his two sisters Dawn, 18, Allison, 13, and two brothers, Marc, 12, and John, 9. The family had owned the property since 1965 after moving to Long Island from Brooklyn where Ronald was born.

Later that evening, at around 6.30pm, Ronald walked into Henry's Bar in Amityville and told anyone who listened that his parents had been shot and that he needed help. The bar was Ronald's local, and his friend Joe Yeswit was inside, who informed Suffolk County Police about the possible shooting.

When they arrived at the house, they found the bodies of all six family members in their bedrooms, face down on the bed. Ronald's parents had been shot twice and his siblings killed with a single bullet to the head. Later autopsies suggested that his mother and sister, Dawn, were alive at the time of the attacks.

Confession

When Ronald told police he suspected the killings might have been carried out by a mafia hitman, he was taken into custody for his own protection. He claimed the hitman was Louis Falini, a local man considered to have connections to the mob but Falini had an alibi showing he was not in Amityville at the time of the shootings.

It would also have been considered unusual for a mafia hitman to have killed someone in their own home, let alone their entire family. When police realised that Ronald was deflecting attention away from himself, they uncovered inconsistencies in his story.

The next day, Ronald confessed to the murders and was escorted back to the house to show investigators how he had killed his family. He claimed the whole incident went by so fast that he couldn't remember all of it.

Ronald took investigators to the locations where he had discarded his bloody clothes and where he had thrown the rifle into the nearby river. He explained how he had taken a bath after the killings, changed into his work clothes and gone to work at the family's car dealership that same day.

While there, Ronald phoned the house wondering why his father hadn't turned up for work. When there was no answer, he left and hung out with friends, telling them that he couldn't reach his family on the phone – an attempt at creating an alibi for the resulting investigation.

When he returned to the house in the evening to find his family dead, he ran to Henry's Bar calling for help. It was an unusual way to have admitted to the murders and more unusual that he had gone to work straight after.

Forged in aggression

The answer to the question of why Ronald had killed his family, lay hidden away in his past. Born 26th September 1951, the firstborn to his parents, he grew up in Brooklyn, New York, and got the nickname 'Butch' due to his size and reputation of fighting with other children and people bigger than himself.

His father was a highly successful car salesman who had worked at his own father's Buick dealership since childhood. As such, he could afford a lavish lifestyle for his family. But the lavishness and middle-class living came at a price.

Ronald Sr. was aggressive and sometimes violent towards his wife and children, with particular attention and abuse aimed at Ronald Jr. who was expected to have followed in his father's footsteps but didn't.

Along with being the target of aggression and physical abuse, Ronald was also bullied at school for the way he looked, though there wasn't anything entirely wrong with him, just that he was larger and meaner than some of the other boys.

During his teenage years, Ronald fought back and lashed out at his schoolfriends and family, even physically attacking his father. When his parents took him to see a psychiatrist, it made Ronald worse, and he would constantly deny that he needed help. Then, in 1965, the family moved to Amityville.

Violence and threats

To placate his violent manner, Ronald's parents showered him with gifts to incentivise good behaviour. When he was 16, he was gifted a speedboat worth $15,000 at the time. However, the appeasements made Ronald worse, and by the age of 17, he was addicted to taking LSD and heroin, two drugs considered the most damaging to an already broken mind.

Still believing they were helping Ronald, his parents continued to bribe him with gifts, including a job at the car dealership. He was also gifted a brand new car, guns, alcohol, and a weekly allowance from his father which he spent on drugs.

At one point during a hunting trip in early 1974, Ronald threatened his friend with the rifle he would later use to kill his family then acted as if nothing had happened, devoid of emotion or recompense. A few weeks later, Ronald interrupted a fight between his parents and pointed the rifle at his father.

When he pulled the trigger, the rifle malfunctioned but his parents were shocked to the core that their son had attempted to kill his father. It was perhaps an unfortunate foreshadowing of the horrors to come.

In October 1974, one month before the murders, Ronald planned a fake robbery with his friend. Ronald had been trusted with taking the car dealership's earnings to the bank, and in late October was due to transport $20,000.

Instead of going to the bank, he and his friend got into a mock fight and 'robbed' the money, which they split 50/50. When police arrived at the dealership, Ronald refused to help their investigation, leading his father to suspect that Ronald was the culprit.

Two weeks before the murders, Ronald threatened to kill his father if he continued to involve police in the robbery. Then, on 13th November, Ronald rampaged through the house and shot dead his entire family.

Voices in his head

One year later in October 1975, Ronald's trial began as his defence put forward an insanity plea. While on the stand, Ronald told the court he'd heard voices in his head that told him to shoot his entire family.

The defence psychiatrist concluded that Ronald was suffering from Dissociative Identity Disorder (DID) and was unable to fully connect with reality. His memories, thoughts, and actions were detached which meant he found it difficult to function in normal everyday life.

DID is rarely associated with violence, but in 1975, it was a different story. We live in a world now where mental health is thankfully better understood and we have the knowledge that disorders require professional help and are not bound to historical sensationalist ideals.

But the prosecution psychiatrists posited a different side to Ronald. They claimed that he had an antisocial personality and was only disconnected from reality due to his extreme use of LSD and heroin. They concluded that Ronald was aware of his actions which existed only to serve his own selfish reality.

The jury in the trial agreed with the prosecution psychiatrists and found Ronald guilty of six counts of murder. In November 1975, Ronald was handed down six consecutive life sentences.

In the years that followed, away from the sensationalism of The Amityville Horror, the case of Ronald DeFeo became even weirder. The biggest question on the lips of journalists and researchers was why. Why did Ronald kill his entire family?

No gunshots were heard

It was no secret that he had a poor relationship with his father and that a plausible motive was to kill him out of anger or revenge. Yet, it didn't explain why Ronald had killed his entire family, including his nine-year-old brother.

All six victims were found face down on their beds and had not been moved after their deaths. Ronald walked through the house with a loud rifle, so it remained unusual that the rest of the family didn't wake up after the first victim was shot.

There was a suspicion that Ronald had drugged them but autopsies showed no signs of anything untoward. The rifle used in the attack had no sound suppressor which meant it would have been loud, with eight bullets used in total.

None of the neighbours heard gunshots with only one claiming they heard the DeFeo's dog barking in the middle of the night. It would have been odd to hear a dog bark and not hear the sound of a rifle going off eight times.

It was suggested that Ronald killed his father for his life insurance and killed his mother so that he would be next in line as the eldest child, but it didn't explain why his four siblings had to die. Then as time went on, Ronald told interviewers three new stories of what he believed really happened.

Tall tales of murder

In a 1986 interview from behind bars, Ronald said that his 18-year-old sister Dawn killed their father.

Upon seeing what she had done, their mother killed Dawn and the rest of Ronald's siblings. When she tried to kill Ronald, he fought back and killed her.

In 1990, Ronald's defence team filed an appeal on the basis of a new story that Ronald had told. He alleged that he was now telling the truth as it was time for the world to hear what really happened and who he had been protecting.

On that fateful night, Ronald claimed an unidentified attacker, who was known to Dawn, killed their parents. Dawn then walked through the house and killed the other three siblings, before turning the gun on Ronald.

Ronald saw the unidentified man flee the house as he and Dawn fought for control of the gun. The gun went off by accident and killed Dawn. Realising what he had done, he positioned the bodies on the bed and tried to come up with a false alibi to protect himself and his dead sister. He stated that he lied, simply to protect his sister.

The appeal was thrown out as the judge found it to be fanciful and full of lies, in attempt to place blame on a long-dead sister who by any account was an innocent victim. And then in 2000, a third story about what 'really' happened, emerged.

The most haunted house in America

26 years after the murders, Ronald was interviewed by author and researcher Ric Osuna. He told Osuna that he was guilty of the murders but that he killed his family in league with Dawn and two of her friends, because their father was plotting to kill him.

When Dawn murdered the other siblings, Ronald became enraged and knocked Dawn out before shooting her in the head. The two people with Dawn had by that point apparently left the house. Forensic experts have since debunked all three stories on the basis of evidence found at the scene.

Ronald died of natural causes in March 2021, with some outlets refusing to release the cause of death, most likely to continue the sensationalist circus built upon the paranormal happenings written about in The Amityville Horror.

In December 1975, one year after the murders and one month after Ronald's conviction, the Lutz family moved into 112 Ocean Avenue. After only 28 days, the family fled the house after being terrorised by paranormal entities.

Three months after they fled, in March 1976, the house was investigated by demonologists and paranormal investigators, Ed and Lorraine

Warren, who are now immortalised in *The Conjuring* movies.

One of their images taken from inside the house shows a young boy with glowing eyes standing at the foot of the main staircase. It has since been used as proof that the house was haunted, whether by the ghosts of the DeFeo family or something far more sinister.

Some paranormal researchers, including the Warren's, believe that Ronald had been possessed by one of the house's demon spirits, and maintain it to be the reason why he went on to kill his family. The voices he heard were put down to possession.

Regardless of one's own beliefs surrounding The Amityville Horror and the DeFeo massacre that came before, the property is still considered one of the most haunted houses in the United States – with no vibrator in sight.

Smelly Bobby Tulip

Robert Black was convicted of four murders but has been linked to at least 21 more, making him one of Britain's most prolific serial killers, with an unusual and disturbing taste for young girls.

There have been many British serial killers but perhaps none more disturbed and horrific than the story of rapist and murderer Robert Black. Black was a paedophile and killer who operated from 1969 to 1987.

He was a truck driver who made regular work trips to mainland Europe where it is suspected he murdered dozens more, and as time has moved on, the links have become more certain.

He was also prime suspect in the infamous 1978 disappearance and murder of 13-year-old Genette Tate, who had vanished on her newspaper delivery round in Devon, on England's Southern Coast. Her murder remains unsolved but linked to Black.

Black was born in Grangemouth, Scotland, in 1947. As his mother didn't know who Robert's father was, she had him adopted soon after and he was taken in by a couple who lived in Kinlochleven, in the Scottish Highlands.

Black went through life with the surname of Tulip, which he took from his adopted parents. He was called 'Smelly Bobby Tulip' by school friends due to his poor hygiene – and the name stuck. When he was growing up, he became an outcast and was prone to outbursts of anger and aggression.

From an early age, Black believed he should have been born a girl, and at five-years-old was caught comparing his genitalia with a girl of the same age. From the age of eight, he would insert objects into his anus and was known to have carried on with the unusual practice into his adulthood.

Disturbed from a young age

Black was knowing to wet the bed on regular occasions, which has been linked as one of the many pre-cursors to violence in later life. Every time he did so, he was beaten by his foster mother and couldn't fight back, resulting in numerous marks and regular bruising on his body.

When he was 11, both his foster parents died from apparent natural causes, and he was adopted by another couple in the small village. In the same year, he dragged a younger girl into a public toilet and attempted to rape her.

Concerned by his violent and abusive behaviour, his new foster parents had him removed from their care to a mixed-sex children's care home near Falkirk on the central belt of Scotland. Straight away, Black tried to abuse some of the girls there and sent to a stricter care home for boys only.

While there, and for the next three years, he was abused himself by a male carer and would regularly be forced to perform oral sex on him. He was also bullied physical and sexually by the other boys despite requiring to be constantly isolated due to his behaviour.

In 1963, when he was 16, he left the care home on his own accord and more into a small flat. He became a delivery boy for a local butcher and manipulated the deliveries so that he could deliver to houses with young girls who were alone. He later claimed to have touched or attacked at least 30 young girls on his deliveries.

In the same year, he lured a seven-year-old girl to an abandoned air-raid shelter then throttled her until she passed out, before masturbating over her body. He was arrested but a psychiatrist's report claimed it was only a one-off and he was let go without punishment.

Black was only 16 at the time and had attempted rape multiple times, been raped himself, and sexually attacked over 30 girls. It should have been clear to psychiatrist's then that Black was an immense danger to society. As it was, he was left to evolve from an abuser to a killer.

First confirmed victim

In 1968, when he was 21, Black moved to London after being released from a borstal on another offence of child abuse. He moved to a bedsit near King's Cross Station where young children were in plentiful supply.

He had multiple jobs, including a life-guard position that he was fired from for sexually touching a young girl – which comes as no surprise in hindsight. He started collecting child pornography through a contact at an illegal book shop in King's Cross.

He later managed to get hold of VHS tapes depicting child abuse. He also covertly took photos of children at swimming pools and in shops and kept the images in locked suitcases, due to the amount of material he had amassed.

He then moved into the attic of a Scottish couple in the area and got himself a long-distance driving job. In his truck he kept various disguises including different types of glasses. He also alternated between having a long beard and no beard at all.

His first confirmed murder victim came when he was 34, in August of 1981. He abducted nine-year-old Jennifer Cardy in Northern Ireland, while on a long-haul journey. She had been riding her bike near to a main road when she vanished.

Hundreds of volunteers joined the search for the girl, and her body was found in a large lake, six days later by two fishermen. Black had brutally raped and drowned the girl. The police suspected the killer might have been a truck driver due to the location of the lake to the trunk road.

Even though it would have been someone who was familiar with the roads around it, no connection was made to Black and his past convictions. It seemed that Black was able to get away with abuse and murder so easily that he ended up incorporating it into his truck routes.

Multiple murders and connections

His second confirmed murder victim was 11-year-old Susan Claire Maxwell, from Cornhill-on-Tweed, close to the Scottish border. Maxwell had been playing sports with friends and walked home alone, before being kidnapped by Black.

300 officers and hundreds more volunteers were involved in the search and an investigation was made of every property in the area, along with a huge amount of open land. A month later, in August of the same year, her decomposed body was found by a lorry driver in a shallow grave at the side of the road. She had been tied up and gagged, with her underwear carefully positioned under her head.

Another three confirmed victims turned up from 1983 to 1987. There were also multiple disappearances and murders that were later linked to Black. In the United Kingdom alone, six more disappearances and murders were attributed to him.

There were also disappearances and murders across Ireland, the Netherlands and Germany. All of the victims vanished or were killed at the same time as Black would have been in the areas on his long-haul European journeys.

A full victim list and linked victim list can be found after the bibliography at the back of this book.

Cutting grass

The nationwide manhunt for Robert Black was one of the most expensive and most resource-heavy UK murder investigations of the 20th century. But he was caught when a member of the public witnessed one of his abductions.

On 14th July 1990, 53-year-old retiree David Herkes was cutting his grass when he saw a blue van slow down on the other side of the road. Herkes started to clean the blades of his lawnmower and happened to look up to see the feet of a small girl lifted from the pavement and into the van.

He watched as Black pushed the girl into the passenger seat before quickly getting in and driving away. Already, Herkes believed he had witnessed an abduction and wrote down the registration number. He realised it might have been the six-year-old daughter of his neighbour and ran to her house where they called the police immediately.

Within minutes the area was covered in police vehicles. A short while passed and Herkes continued to describe what had happened to officers. Suddenly, Black had decided to drive back through the town on his way northwards and Herkes recognised the van instantly.

He shouted to officers who jumped in front of the van and pulled Black from his seat. The father of the missing girl charged into the van and found his daughter tied up in a sleeping bag. She had already been sexually abused but had survived and would go on to make a full recovery. It was the last child that Black would ever touch.

Prime suspect

In 1994, Black was convicted of the rape and murder of three girls, along with kidnapping and sexual assault. He received a sentence of life imprisonment with a minimum of 35 years. The case caused outrage in the United Kingdom and saw protests calling for the death penalty to be reinstated in the country.

Up until his death, he was charged with another murder from 1981 and was about to be charged with more when he died of a heart attack in January 2016. He was already a prime suspect in most of his suspected victims.

Robert Black remains one of the worst serial killers to walk the streets of the United Kingdom and

Europe. Not only was his brutality unheard of in the British Isles at the time, but the huge number of lives he affected was never forgotten.

The unusual aspect of the Robert Black case is that many unsolved murders and disappearances of young girls across the United Kingdom and Europe in the 1980s and 1990s, continue to be linked to him.

Many feel that Black has become a catch-all name for many local police forces to use for 'solving' unsolved cases. Not unlike Henry Lee Lucas in the United States, when at one point in time, over 3,000 murders were attributed him, clearing the unsolved slate of many local law enforcement agencies.

Due to his extensive travelling and number of disappearance on his truck routes, it is possible that Black was one of the most prolific serial killers ever to walk the British Isles and Europe. But with his passing, Smell Bobby Tulip has taken his numerous secrets to the grave.

One Infamous Murder & Seven Suspects

One infamous murder, seven suspects, infinite theories. You are dared to tread through a real-life horror story that has haunted and taunted investigators for quarter-of-a-century.

One of the most infamous cases in all of true crime history is the unsolved Christmas murder of American child beauty queen, JonBenét Patricia Ramsey. Get your web-sleuthing notepad at the ready and kick back in Agatha Christie mode.

On Boxing Day 1996, in Boulder, Colorado, six-year-old JonBenét was reported missing. Seven hours later, her body was discovered in the basement of her family home. She had a fractured skull caused by a heavy blow and had been strangled by a garrotte around her neck.

An autopsy showed she had died of strangulation and cranial trauma. A murder investigation began that generated worldwide interest, the likes of which had rarely been seen before. A quarter-of-a-century later, JonBenét's untimely death remains in the spotlight.

Over the years, the death of the blue-eyed pageant queen has taunted and haunted true crime investigators, due to conflicting theories, false confessions, a growing body of evidence, and misdirection at all levels.

Some believe she was accidentally killed by a family member who then staged her death to look like a kidnapping gone wrong. Others believe an intruder broke into the family home and killed her. While some suspect there was a collusion between family members to rid themselves of her.

Here, we take a brief look at the details of the case and offer up all possible suspects so that you, dear reader, can form your own conclusions as to who may have killed the child beauty queen.

Child beauty queen

JonBenét was born in 1990 to wealthy parents Patricia and John Ramsey, in Atlanta, Georgia. The family moved shortly after to Colorado, where JonBenét went to school. John was the president of a successful computer software company whose headquarters were based in Colorado.

He had amassed a large amount of wealth and was well-respected within his business community. Patricia was a lady of leisure who took beauty pageants seriously enough to enter JonBenét into various competitions around Colorado, from the age of four.

Patricia developed a pageant-mother attitude that rubbed people up the wrong way but it saw JonBenét win various contests including America's Royale Miss, Little Miss Colorado, Colorado State All-Star Kids Cover Girl, and National Tiny Miss Beauty.

Unsurprisingly, media coverage of JonBenét's death focused heavily on the beauty pageant aspect of her life, which was heavily criticised by reporters from international newspapers. This led to the Ramsey family filing multiple suits against media outlets, something that probably didn't help the investigation.

Late on Christmas night in 1996, Patricia returned home to find her daughter missing, and a long handwritten ransom note on the kitchen staircase. The ransom was set at precisely $118,000 (USD), which was bizarrely identical to John's bonus the year before.

The note said to not contact the police or friends, but Patricia called the police in the early hours of Boxing Day morning. Two officers arrived and did a basic search of the house but didn't go into the basement as it was locked from the outside, which meant any burglar or kidnapper could not have used that exit.

They found no signs of forced entry and took statements from Patricia and John. A forensic team arrived at the large property and worked on the basis that JonBenét had been kidnapped – still no-one had searched the basement.

Contamination

John began planning to pay the ransom while forensics were going through JonBenét's bedroom in minute detail. The team only cordoned off the bedroom which meant the rest of the house became contaminated all too easily, with friends and other family members arriving throughout the morning.

Almost all the visitors left their fingerprints on the surfaces and items in the house, which would prove to be one of the case's downfalls as time went on. A detective arrived and started looking at religious sources, on the basis that the $118,000 ransom was linked to Psalm 118 – it wasn't.

Hours had passed, and still, no-one had bothered to check the basement. Then, seven hours after the 911 call had been made, at 1pm, a detective asked John to search the house to see if anything was missing. He and a friend, Fleet White, began their search in the basement.

It was there, where they found the body of his daughter. JonBenét's mouth was covered with duct tape, her wrists tied and her body covered with a white blanket. John picked up the body and took it back upstairs, further contaminating the crime scene. It was then the case went from a missing person to a homicide investigation.

Patricia and John provided handwriting samples, blood, and hair samples, and were interviewed by police extensively. With the contamination of evidence, the police were already struggling to come up with a motive and a walk-through of what actually happened.

For the first two weeks after the body was discovered, the police interviewed as many people as they could and tried to piece together the crime scene. But as weeks turned into months, and months into years, the chances of securing a suspect remained low.

But with the huge amount of media interest and as one of the first cases to be taken on by internet armchair sleuths, a number of suspects and theories have come to light over the years. Let's dive in.

The Mother

Patricia, and indeed John, were officially exonerated in 2008 due to advances in DNA technology, however, they still rise to the top of the suspect list due to the circumstances of the death and inconsistencies between them.

Patricia was the one who found the ransom note on the stairs, but it wasn't an ordinary ransom note. At almost three pages long, it read more like it would in the films, than a genuine attempt to extort money from the wealthy.

In almost all ransom cases, the note is short and to the point, it doesn't need to be anything else. This led to the suspicion that Patricia had written the letter herself in a different handwriting style. The note was written on a few sheets of Patricia's own notebook and written using her own pen.

It is suspected she did this on the basis that she accidentally killed JonBenét. JonBenét was known to still be bedwetting and this angered Patricia every time. Though she had never shown signs of violence toward her daughter, there is the suggestion that she hit JonBenét hard enough to cause damage.

Believing she had killed her, she finished the job in the basement and used a garrotte fashioned from paintbrushes taken from her own paint kit near to where the body was found. As with John, it stands to reason they would have locked the basement from the outside.

The case against Patricia, is that she was never violent or physically aggressive against anyone. In historical cases, many parents who accidentally kill their own children would either own up to it or try to hide the body away from the location of the crime.

In this instance, JonBenét was simply placed in the basement. An elaborate scheme of kidnapping and ransom may have been too far-fetched for either parent to come up with. But if it was a real kidnapping then it was a mystery why the kidnappers left the child in the house.

The Father

When asked to search the house, John and his friend went immediately to the basement where they found the body. Some suggest he went there because he knew the body was there, however it's more likely he began the search there as it was the lowest level in the house.

He immediately picked up the body without saying anything, either accidentally or deliberately contaminating the body. He removed the duct tape and wrapped her in a wool blanket in the lounge, destroying any evidence along the way.

The detective on scene at the time, noted that both parents were aware the ransom note said 10am at the latest on Boxing Day morning. But as 10am came and went, both parents didn't seem to worry too much about the deadline passing.

The detective later said that she was so sure the killer was still in the house, she counted the number of bullets in her holster, just in case. Another officer overheard John talking on the phone about booking flights to Atlanta, which would be an unusual thing to do, seeing as his daughter was missing.

Aside from false rumours of sexual abuse that did the circuits a decade later, there was no solid evidence on which to charge Patricia or John. Though many had a feeling that at least one of the pair were involved somehow.

The Brother

Burke Ramsay, who was nine-years-old at the time was protected from the press by his parents for many years. For that reason alone, theories began to develop in the media and online forums.

When police arrived Boxing Day morning, on the kitchen worktop was a half-eaten bowl of pineapple snacks. When the autopsy on JonBenét was carried out, she had undigested pineapple in her stomach, though rarely ate it.

On the kitchen counter was also a heavy square flashlight that was only noticed in crime scene photos many years later. The theory goes that Burke was eating his pineapple when JonBenét took some from his bowl, this angered Burke who grabbed the flashlight and hit her over the head.

Upon seeing what he had done, his parents covered up the death and staged it to look like a kidnapping. FBI profilers later questioned Burke but found no evidence to suggest he had accidentally killed her. Except the flashlight was square, and the indentation on JonBenét's head was also square.

Later DNA tests showed there was no trace evidence of JonBenét or Burke on the flashlight. But any trace evidence could have been wiped clean before it was tested. However, the flashlight theory has never really gone away.

JonBenét had strange marks on her back, which were similar to those of Burke's toy train track. The suggestion there was that he prodded her to see if she was alive. As an adult, Burke maintains his innocence and has sued multiple media agencies for defamatory statements.

The Teacher

With any high-profile case, it is somewhat inevitable that a false confession would be given from someone seeking attention or infamy. In 2006, former schoolteacher, John Mark Karr, did just that, though some suspect he may in fact have been telling the truth.

Karr had already eloped to Thailand after facing charges of possession of child porn in the United States. When he read a documentary was being made on the JonBenét murder, he reached out to the filmmaker and confessed the killing in graphic sexual detail.

Karr was arrested in Bangkok and extradited to Colorado where he would face charges of killing JonBenét. It became clear that he had a sick fascination with the six-year-old, including having stored images of her from the beauty pageants on his computer.

However, there was no DNA evidence linking him to the crime at all, despite his very detailed method of how he killed her. It was believed that he was seeking notoriety and infamy and gave a false confession to achieve it. He was convicted on child porn charges and released a couple of years later.

The Housekeeper

The Ramsey's employed a housekeeper named Linda Hoffman-Pugh who had a key to the home. Her husband was also a handyman for the property. Patricia claimed that Linda was struggling for money and asked to borrow thousands of dollars, which Patricia declined.

Linda was interviewed by police the day after the body was found, had handwriting samples taken, along with fingerprints and strands of hair. The theory was that she took JonBenét into the basement to hide her so she could get the funds from the ransom.

As the Ramsey's housekeeper, she was closely connected with them, knew their schedules inside out, knew the layout of the house intricately, and also didn't have a solid alibi the night of the murder. Linda later rebutted the accusations and placed the blame squarely on Patricia.

She claimed that Patricia had multiple personalities which had never been detected by medical professionals. Patricia would be a caring mother one moment, then an angry overbearing parent the next. Needless to say, Linda was quickly fired as housekeeper.

The Drifter

A 32-year-old town drifter named Gary Oliva was suspected to be the killer by the Ramsey's private investigator, Ollie Gray. Oliva was a known sex offender and convicted paedophile who was living in the area at the time of the murder.

He was arrested in 2000 on drug charges, and in his backpack, police found a magazine cut-out of JonBenét. Gray was so adamant that Oliva was the killer that he publicly ridiculed the police department for not considering Oliva as a suspect.

One of Oliva's high-school friends, Michael Vail, claimed that Oliva had phoned him to confess about hurting a little girl, just days after JonBenét was found. According to Vail, the knot used in the garrotte around JonBenét's neck, was similar to the one used in an incident where Oliva choked his own mother.

The strange marks on JonBenét's back, thought to have been caused by Burke's toy train track, may have been caused by a stun-gun, which Oliva was known to carry with him everywhere he went. Oliva was cleared on the basis that the DNA evidence didn't match. Despite that, he was later charged and convicted in a separate offence with possessing child porn.

Santa Claus

The final suspect to have been banded around the case, is Bill McReynolds, who was known as the town's Santa. One week before the murder, Bill was entertaining children at a party being held by Patricia at the Ramsey residence.

Dressed as Santa Claus, he was known to have paid special attention to JonBenét and stated that he would pay her a secret visit at Christmas. It was claimed that he had chosen her to be his special friend. JonBenét gave him a gift of gold glitter, which he took into heart surgery with him many months later.

He also requested his wife to mix the glitter into his ashes when he died, such was the connection he felt with JonBenét. Though many believe the friendly neighbourhood Santa was completely innocent, there are some who are adamant he was the killer.

Bill knew the property well, was acquainted with JonBenét as part of their special friendship, and was trusted by the Ramsey's, and indeed other children's families in the town. But again, there was no evidence to connect him to the murder, beyond circumstantial.

Pieces on a board

The JonBenét murder has long played out like a game of Cluedo, where suspects and evidence are offered up for the inner detective in all of us to decide. What's first important is the motive. Who would gain from murdering her?

On the motive side, it seems rather obvious to point out that a child beauty queen, paraded around the State of Colorado to rapturous applause, would garner the attention of child sex offenders. It would have been easy to find out where she lived, due to the stature and wealth of the family.

On the night she was killed, two windows had been left open to access wires for the outdoor Christmas lights. The window in the basement was broken and hadn't yet been fixed. However, when officers first arrived at the house, they noted the basement was locked from the outside, which is why they didn't enter.

This meant that whoever put JonBenét in the basement had locked it behind them and exited the house from the inside. It would seem like an awful lot of trouble and risk to go to, instead of exiting through the broken window in the basement.

The foliage had not been broken or damaged around the outside of the basement window which meant the killer had gone back into the main house. Many detectives believe the killer had broken into the house, stunned JonBenét, took her to the basement, killed her, and left a ransom note.

Leaving a ransom note implies that financial gain was the motive for the murder. However, it seems unlikely that a kidnapper would leave their hostage inside the place they had taken them from. More than often, the hostage or victim is removed from a location to be held until ransom is paid.

Which is why the ransom note becomes more of a focal point in retellings of this case. If JonBenét was abused by a sex offender and killed then there would have been evidence of abuse – which was never uncovered. Yet it doesn't mean that she wasn't abused, it just means there was no evidence.

A case for the ages

In the months before the murder, there had been over 100 burglaries in the area, and 38 registered sex-offenders lived within two miles of the house. But police found no signs that the house had been broken into.

The consensus among most researchers is that an intruder was responsible for JonBenét's death. Yet, the case is seemingly stuck in the void, a story that remains far from being solved. There are too many inconsistencies and questions that it's no wonder there are many books filled with information about it.

We end, quite unfortunately with the schoolteacher, John Karr, who it was claimed had given a false confession. What he did afterwards would either confirm his quest for notoriety, or prove he was in fact telling the truth.

In 2010, Karr was discovered to be putting together a child sex cult called '*The Immaculates*'. His vision was to create a cult of JonBenét lookalikes who would bend to his every will. He claimed that his disciples needed to be blond, with small feet, and from the age of four upwards.

It turned out, he had even married a 13-year-old girl in the 1980s. One of his followers was a 19-year-old girl who got to know him when she was a nine-year-old pupil at the school he taught at. She later confessed that he beat her and forced her to recruit girls who looked like JonBenét. She was later rescued by her parents and sent to a rehabilitation facility for 18 months to break her connection with him.

That Karr was able to get away with something like this, proves he was more than just pushing forward an ideal of himself, more than the infamy he sought. Though he may not have been involved in the death of JonBenét, he is evidence of the evil that permeates through to our everyday lives.

Seven suspects remain at the forefront of the case, despite all being cleared through DNA evidence; the mother, the father, the brother, the teacher, the housekeeper, the drifter, and Santa Claus. Or perhaps there is a mystery person who has never been considered.

Wherever you stand on the JonBenét case, it is a Christmas horror story that Boulder has never been allowed to forget, of a young girl whose life was ended in such a cruel fashion. For hers is a name that echoes in infamy as one of America's most scandalous unsolved murders.

The Wedding Day Murders

While he was on the run from the law, a notorious criminal murdered three members of the same family, kickstarting a 39-day manhunt.

Arthur Hutchinson's penchant for violence began at an early age. At just seven-years-old, he took a knife to his younger sister and stabbed her. It began a life of crime that ended with triple murder in a village in Sheffield.

Born during the middle of the Second World War on 19th February 1941, Arthur was raised by his mother, Louise, who would constantly claim he was her favourite son. He and his half-brother, Dino, were raised on a rundown Hartlepool, County Durham, housing estate.

Louise believed Arthur could do no wrong and felt protective over him, despite his predilection for petty crime, even from a young age. Yet, many of

Arthur's friends simply believed he was trying to prove something to his peers, as he was constantly being picked on at school.

Whenever he did something wrong, he ran back to Louise, who would forgive him for his wrongdoings, which meant Arthur would constantly be getting away with crime. By the age of 17, Arthur was already known to the police for car theft and had been given community sentences multiple times.

Life after the Second World War in England was difficult for many, not least because of the economic downturn, but many children lost their fathers, and wives; their husbands. Arthur was one of those affected by the fallout of the war but he chose a life of crime.

According to Dino, Arthur wasn't shy with the girls, and due to his bad boy image, had girls lining up around the corner to be with him. But the police saw Arthur a little differently. They suspected he was a predator who was building his criminal career purely to show off and make himself look powerful.

Arthur's work colleagues and friends feared he would escalate to bigger crimes, and they were right. From his mid-twenties, Arthur began sexually assaulting women and carrying firearms around the streets, before escalating to triple murder.

Wedding Day

In the 1970s, Arthur was convicted of a number of sexual assaults, and the attempted murder of Dino. For the attempt on his half-brother's life, Arthur was sentenced to five years but freed in 1983. In late September of that year, Arthur was arrested again on suspicion of burglary and rape.

While in the police station, he asked to use the restroom on the second floor then jumped out of the window. He miscalculated the distance and height of the jump and sliced his knees open on the barbed wire fence surrounding the station.

For the next three weeks, Arthur went on the run, living in the wilds and becoming homeless to avoid detection. He claimed he avoided police helicopters and searches by hiding in dense bushes and large water drains. But after three weeks, he needed a better place to hide.

On 23rd October 1983, the Laitner family had spent the day celebrating the wedding of their daughter Suzanne to Scottish optician Ivor Wolfe. The gathering was held at the Laitner family home in Dore, Sheffield, a village with a population of around 5,500.

That evening, once the party had ended, and the marquee in the garden was clear, four members of the Laitner family remained in the large house. 59-year-old Basil Laitner, his wife, 55-year-old Avril, their 28-year-old son Richard, and 18-year-old daughter Nicola.

Arthur had planned to burgle the house as he had been watching it from afar and expected little resistance from the Laitner family. He broke in through the rear patio door and came face to face with Richard, who he stabbed multiple times, leaving him to die in a pool of his own blood.

Basil heard the commotion and began walking down the stairs to see what was going on. As he got to the top of the landing, Arthur stabbed him three times and pushed his lifeless body down the stairs. Then, the women of the house realised what was going on.

Massacre

Avril attempted to fight Arthur off by grabbing the knife but the blade sliced her fingers to the bone before she too was stabbed to death. He then grabbed Nicola by the hair and forced her to the top of the house at knifepoint, stepping over the body of her father in the process.

In her bedroom, Nicola was tied up and raped multiple times. As Arthur knelt on Nicola's bed, the wound on his damaged knee opened up and bled onto the sheets, something that would later help prove he was the culprit of the crimes.

He left Nicola tied up on the bed before retreating to the kitchen and helping himself to leftovers from the wedding reception, including champagne and upmarket cheese. For a reason that has never been explained, he left Nicola tied up but alive, and left the house in the early hours of the morning.

It's possible he had drunk so much champagne that he simply forgot to kill Nicola or thought himself so invincible that he would never be caught. He eloped off into the night and was about to become Britain's most wanted man.

The following morning, workmen with the marquee company showed up to dismantle the structure when they found Nicola covered in blood. Police were called immediately, who discovered the bloodbath that Arthur had left.

With Nicola suffering from a complete psychological collapse and becoming catatonic for many days, the police had a huge task on their hands. The wedding day killings, as it become known in the press, was one of the first major cases in the UK to use new video technology to record the scene in detail.

But they had one major problem, with Nicola unable to talk, they had a list of near 400 suspects, all of whom attended the wedding party. This was in addition to the peripheral people involved such as caterers, the marquee company, and everything else that went along with a wedding.

And yet, three days later, with the help of professional police psychologists, Nicola was able to provide a perfect description of Arthur to the police. When they saw the artist's sketch, they knew exactly who was responsible for the wedding day massacre.

The Fox

Despite having the killer's blood on the sheet and his handprint on the champagne bottle, it proved of little use in the days before DNA testing and computerised databases. Which is why Nicola's witness statement proved vital to capturing Arthur.

For the next 39 days, a national manhunt ensued to capture Arthur, and his photo was on the front page of every newspaper in the country, both national and local. He first hid in the woodland of Worksop, 19 miles east of Sheffield.

After a few days, Arthur believed the manhunt was dying down and he began staying at guesthouses and pubs in and around Barnsley, Nottinghamshire. At every accommodation, he used a different disguise, from items he had stolen along the way.

He also began writing letters to the police and newspapers, claiming he was not responsible for the massacre, and that someone else had orchestrated the whole thing. In the letters, he referred to himself as 'The Fox'.

There was one aspect of Arthur's case that made him predictable, and it was one the police used to their advantage. Arthur always returned home to his mother, Louise, who in the early days at least, would forgive him for his crimes.

Detectives tapped Louise's telephone line in secret, and in early November, they got the call they were waiting for. Arthur had phoned his mother from a public telephone box to inform her he was coming home and would arrive on bonfire night, the 5th of November.

On that cold, misty, and historically important day, hundreds of police and dogs flooded the woodland around the estate which Arthur was trying to make his way back to. They believed the woods was the only possible way Arthur could take in and out of the estate, due to the amount of hiding places.

As the evening drew in on 5th November, a local farmer named George Bailes returned to the farmhouse after checking on his cattle. His wife frantically pulled him to one side, claiming she had seen Arthur making his way across their farm.

When police were informed of his likely location, they descended on the woodland around the Bailes farm, forcing Arthur into a dense thicket. Realising the dogs were closing in, Arthur fled the woods with his knife out in front of him, in one last ditch attempt to reach his mother's home.

Life tariff

Unsurprisingly, the dogs caught up to him first, and pushed him to the ground. In a fitting twist of fate, Arthur attempted to stab one of the dogs but missed and plunged the knife into himself. Unable to move, Arthur was arrested and taken to hospital in an ambulance, bringing an end to the large 39-day manhunt.

His mother was allowed to see him in hospital, but later told reporters that she did not recognise him as her son. Not least for the crimes he had committed but also due to the way his appearance had changed so much when he was on the run.

During his trial the following year in September 1984, Arthur accused many other people of the murders, including a reporter from the Daily Mirror. But the evidence against him was overwhelming, bolstered by the testimony of brave survivor Nicola.

On 14th September, Arthur was found guilty of three murders and one rape and sentenced to life with a minimum term of 18 years. Just weeks after the sentence, which caused outrage among the British public, the Home Secretary applied a whole life tariff, meaning Arthur would never be released.

24 years later, in 2008, Arthur made an appeal against the life tariff, claiming it was a breach of his human rights but the appeal was rejected. Three more appeals in 2013, 2015, and 2017, also failed, and Arthur was condemned to spend the rest of his days in prison.

He Chose To Kill on Saturday Nights

A Welsh serial killer who raped and killed three girls in Port Talbot in 1973 on Saturday nights, was caught 30 years later – after his death – in the first case in history solved using familial DNA testing.

There are very few Welsh serial killers but one who always tops the list is Joseph William Kappen, AKA: The Saturday Night Strangler, so called as he claimed his victims on Saturday nights across Port Talbot in 1973.

He was additionally linked to the unsolved murder of 23-year-old Maureen Mulcahy in Aberavon in 1976, who had left friends to meet an unidentified acquaintance. Her strangled body was found in woodland the next day. Her murder remains unsolved and is still a cold case in Wales.

Kappen is so notorious in Wales that he was the country's first most documented serial killer but as fate would have it, he wouldn't be caught until after his death, when familial DNA testing linked him to the murders, the first time in history it had been used to identify a serial killer and solve a case.

Kappen was born in 1941 and remained in Port Talbot for most of his life. He was raised by his stepfather after his parents split up and was one of seven siblings. Due to the fallout from his parent's divorce, he turned to petty crime, and by the age of 13 was already known to local police for a number of minor thefts.

Into his late teens and early twenties, he garnered over thirty convictions for theft, burglary, and assault, and would spend most of his formative years in and out of prison. He could never hold down a job for longer than a few months and was known as a loner.

When he was 21, he met 17-year-old Christine Powell and they married two years later. Ten days after the marriage, Kappen was sent to prison for burglary. When he was released a few months later, Kappen became abusive and would abuse and rape Christine on many occasions, a sign of things to come.

They had a daughter and son together but it didn't stop Kappen from continuing to abuse his younger wife. At one point, while walking the family dog, he strangled it to death in front of his son, claiming that death was the only way, as the dog was old.

Despite his marriage, Kappen found himself attracted to young teenage girls, who he could project his controlling influence onto. He got a job as a bouncer at local bars and clubs which put him in direct contact with them.

In 1964, after being released from a burglary sentence, he sexually assaulted a 15-year-old girl but she was able to fight him off and escape, but Kappen wasn't identified as the attacker and he was free to search for his first murder victim.

In early 1973, a few months before the murders, Kappen picked up two female hitchhikers then drove them to an isolated lane where he attempted to rape them. They too managed to escape but didn't report it, which led to Kappen moving from attempted rape to murder in order to get what he wanted.

On Saturday 14th July 1973, 16-year-old Sandra Newton and her friends went out drinking in Briton Ferry, a small town in Port Talbot. They visited the local nightclub but got split up, and by the end of the night, Sandra found herself needing a lift back home.

Realising it was a perfect time to hunt for young girls, Kappen found Sandra hitchhiking on the side of the road and lured her into his car. He drove her to the grounds of a rural coal mine a few miles away, dragged her out of the car and raped her before strangling her to death with her own skirt.

Kappen didn't attempt to hide the body and dumped Sandra near a water tunnel close to the coal mine. Her body was found three days later, sparking a murder investigation that simply went nowhere. Police suspected the man was local due to having knowledge of the water tunnel but could not pin down a suspect.

Two months later, 16-year-old friends Geraldine Hughes and Pauline Floyd went out clubbing in Swansea, ten miles away from Port Talbot. At that time in history, the term serial killer was still to become public knowledge, and the girls assumed that the murder of Sandra was a one-off that wouldn't happen to anyone else. They were wrong.

After visiting a number of local bars, they went to the Top Rank nightclub in the city and danced through the night until the early hours, when instead of getting a taxi back home, they decided to hitchhike to save money.

Kappen, who was stalking the streets for his victims, noticed the two girls needing a lift and gladly obliged. He drove them to Llandarcy woods, in-between Swansea and Port Talbot, where he raped both girls and strangled them to death.

Their bodies were found the next morning, and when word got around about the double murder, the community recoiled in fear, as three girls had been killed in the same manner within three months, leading police to believe they had a multiple murderer on their hands.

The investigation learned that both girls were seen getting into a white Austin 1100 which became the focus early on in the case. 150 detectives were brought in to work on the case, and they quickly learned there were an estimated 10,000 male drivers of an Austin 1100 within fifty miles of Port Talbot.

In the days before mobile phones and internet, the command room became swamped in paperwork, making the investigation even more difficult, as some of the detectives ended up redoing work that had already been carried out.

After the Austin 1100, the investigation turned to the giant Port Talbot steelworks, where at least 13,000 men were employed. Every single one of them became a suspect, as most local men worked at the factories.

But at the same time, the nearby M4 motorway was under construction, and many of the crew working on it came from outside the area. There was also the possibility that the killer could have come to town to visit the large annual Neath Fair, which took place the weekend of the murders.

Suddenly, the suspect list grew and grew, and with minimal databasing techniques in place, the investigation began to collapse in on itself, which wasn't helped by the miner's strikes that had forced the government to implement a three-day working week.

During the enquiries relating to the Austin 1100, Kappen's name came up as an owner, and police went to his home to interview him. However, Kappen had removed the wheels of the car to make it look as though it was not roadworthy.

Kappen was reported driving the car at the time of the murders but due to the investigation overload, the report wasn't cross-referenced, and in addition to his wife giving him a false alibi out of fear of his abuse, Kappen was struck off the suspect's list.

By the summer of 1974, the investigation came to an end and the hundreds of boxes of paperwork, admin, and evidence, went into storage at Sandfields police station in Port Talbot. 16 years later in 1990, Dr. Colin Dark of the Chepstow's

Forensic Science Services was put on the case, but when he went to visit the storage room, the files had been mostly destroyed by damp and a mice infestation.

Clark was able to anticipate the rise of DNA technology and requested that the physical evidence, including the girl's underwear, should be removed and stored at the Chepstow laboratories for future investigation. It was something that would ultimately solve the case.

In 1998, 25 years after the double murder, technology advanced to such a degree that a male fingerprint was found on the underwear which contained genetic material. Two years later in 2000, Clark and his team began searching the national DNA database. The DNA database was set up in 1995 for people arrested on suspicion of a crime or charged with a crime.

If the killer had been arrested or charged since 1995, then his DNA would show up on the system – but it didn't. Due to having the killer's DNA, the original investigation was fully reopened as a cold case that went under the banner of Operation Magnum.

Three ageing detectives took on the case and were tasked with going back through the mouldy evidence, and at the same time, forensic evidence proved that the killer of the two girls also killed Sandra, and they were linked as three murders for the first time.

The operation got their suspect list down to 500 people, out of 35,000 initial suspects, with help from psychological profiles. Due to the difficulty in tracking down the 500 men, due to the age of the facts the team had on record, only 353 were ever tested but none of them matched the DNA.

Kappen was on the list but had died of lung cancer in June 1990. In 2002, the team used a new DNA tactic called familial genetic testing, which assumes family members will have partial matches of the same DNA. They ran it through the new system and found a car thief named Paul Kappen, who was only seven at the time of the murders.

Realising Joseph Kappen was Paul's father, he became the prime suspect. After Kappen's ex-wife and his daughter gave the investigation DNA swabs, the investigation concluded they had found their killer. The Saturday Night Strangler had been caught – after his death.

In the summer of 2002, almost 30 years after the murders, Kappen's body was exhumed and tested, providing a 100% match for the DNA of the killer. In the case of Maureen Mulcahy, who was killed in 1976, there was no DNA material available which could prove either way if Kappen had killed her, but he has long remained the prime suspect, meaning he might have killed at least four young girls.

The Kappen investigation was the first in the world to use familial DNA tracing to identify a killer and solve a previously unsolved murder. The way the case was solved, led to many other cold cases being cracked, and the technology was implemented across the world.

The Slave Master Killer

By day he was a Sunday School teacher and director of a charity, loved by his community, by night he was the slave master, the first internet serial killer who enslaved and butchered at least six victims.

In the 1970s, porn was a relatively new thing, at least to the mainstream masses. Amateur photography was on the increase and VHS was about to make its mark on history. It wouldn't have been easy to find porn back in the 1970s.

The likes of Ted Bundy and Dennis Radar said it had influenced their outlook on women and was a contributing factor in both of their cases. Heading into the 1990s, it was one of the biggest industries in the world and still remains one of the most searched for terms on the internet.

It was relatively mild images that influenced the likes of Bundy and other serial killers. They used their own imagination to fuel their fantasies, using certain images only as a marker in their mind's eye. With the availability of the internet, there is no need for imagination.

Every type of porn; bizarre or degrading, is instantly available to every age group on any device, anywhere in the world. The days of soft-core true detective magazines are still with us but they pale in comparison to the vast amount of violent pornography that fills over half of the known internet.

Internet anonymity has afforded people with dark thoughts to talk to others about their fantasies or use social media to spark up dehumanising conversations. Some comments underneath degrading images might leave one struggling to see any resemblance of the ethical and moral society we believed we lived in.

It can change their outlook on other people, sexual relations, and the way they perceive the world. Yet, some people use the internet for far darker purposes.

Serial killer John Edward Robinson was the first known person to have exclusively used internet chatrooms as a way to solicit his victims.

Forger

Robinson was a life-time criminal, involved in kidnapping, forgery, assaults, and murder. He was convicted of eight murders but remains connected to others. All his post-1993 victims came from online chatrooms, leading him to be known as the first internet serial killer.

Born in 1943 Illinois, he and his four siblings were raised by an alcoholic father and strict mother. In 1957 he was enrolled at a private boys school for those wishing to become priests.

Just one year later, he was removed from the school due to untold behavioural issues. He then enrolled in medical school but dropped out after two years. It seemed that Robinson was unable to stick to one school or job, a trait that would carry him through life.

By his Twenties, Robinson realised that he was able to manipulate and leech off others. Specifically in the area of forgery, he found it easy to scam other people out of their money and belongings. Aged 21 in 1964, he moved to Kansas City and married Nancy Jo Lynch, who gave birth to four of his children.

Robinson was first arrested in 1969 after forging over $30,000 (USD) from a medical practice where he worked as an X-ray technician. He was convicted of embezzlement and given a three-year suspended sentence.

A scoundrel's life

Up until 1975, he was connected with two more frauds in different companies across various States, with a fraudulent company he had set up. The arrests and sentences he kept on receiving were no deterrent to someone who thrived on forging everything from letters to financial documents.

By 1980, he was becoming well-known around his Kansas City community by involving himself in every possible venture he could. He became a local baseball coach, a Sunday School teacher, and a director of a community charity group.

While working with the charity, he forged letters to the Kansas City Mayor and other political influencers, praising his own voluntary efforts and community spirit. He even named himself Man of the Year within the charity and put on a dinner to celebrate himself. His desire for power was becoming all too evident.

Later in 1980, Robinson was arrested yet again on multiple forgery charges and spent 60 days in prison in 1982. When he was released, he set up another fake company and swindled people out of their money. He claimed it was for his wife's medical care as she was seriously ill – which she wasn't.

At the same time, he was known to be approaching neighbours and local women in his community for sex, some of which gave into his charm and confidence. Some of the women later claimed he had a penchant for violence during sex.

International Council of Masters

In the mid-1980s, Robinson claimed to have joined a cult called the International Council of Masters. It was a secret BDSM cult, whose mission was to lure young women to be tortured and raped by the cult members. He had become the self-titled slave master of the group.

The group itself may have been a spin-off from underground porn, which had taken off ever since VHS had been introduced. Though there are now internet sites and forums with the same name, the original council of masters has never been discovered – if it existed at all.

In 1984, he set up another company and hired 19-year-old Paula Godfrey, to work in sales. He then sent her away for *'training'*. After a few days, Paula's parents reported her missing, and Robinson claimed he had no idea what had happened to her.

A few days later, her parents received a letter from their daughter claiming that she was okay but did not want to see anyone again. Her parents told police the handwriting did not belong to their daughter but the police had nothing else to go on.

They stopped their investigation as the letter was believed by them to be real. Yet, no trace of Paula was ever found, dead or alive, and it is suspected that she was Robinson's first murder victim. He never revealed what had happened to Paula.

Forger to killer

In 1985, he met Lisa Stasi at a women's refuge. He offered her a job and took her away, again for *'training'*. Lisa had a four-month-old daughter who intrigued him, not for himself but for a family member, and a sick plan entered his mind.

Robinson contacted his brother who had been unable to adopt a baby and claimed he was able to *'get hold of one'* on the cheap and through official sources. He forged documents and solicited over $5,000 for legal fees. He then handed the child over to his unsuspecting brother along with the forged papers.

Lisa vanished and was never seen again. She too became a victim of the internet's first serial killer. Later, in 2000, the child was tested, and DNA confirmed she was the daughter of Lisa.

Then in 1987, Robinson hired 27-year-old Catherine Clampitt for a fake job. She vanished a few weeks later and was never seen again. His bogus companies were becoming an avenue through which he could hire his victim of choice.

Yet, he kept on breaking the law in full sight of the authorities. After breaking his probation and being arrested again for multiple fraud incidents, he was sentenced to various prison sentences in Kansas and Missouri. From 1987 to 1993, he remained incarcerated on various charges.

But upon his release, Robinson discovered something that changed the way he selected his victims; the internet.

Chatrooms

Though he had seemingly been disgraced in the community, he still believed himself to be the Man of the Year and carried on with his criminal activity as if it were second nature. While searching the internet, still in its infancy, he found sex and BDSM chatrooms.

He used the growing BDSM chatroom culture to look for women who enjoyed submissive sex. Robinson went by the name of Slavemaster, and after months of the right kind of solicitation, he found a 45-year-old woman named Sheila Faith.

He pretended to be a wealthy businessperson and offered to help pay for her disabled daughter's healthcare. In 1994, Sheila and her 15-year-old wheelchair-bound daughter, vanished from the face of the earth. Robinson carried on forging their documents and received pension and disability cheques for another seven years.

By 1999, Slavemaster was well-known within the growing online BDSM community, who were unaware of his real identity and motives. In the same year he solicited 21-year-old Polish immigrant Izabela Lewicka, after meeting her online.

She claimed she wanted a BDSM relationship and the Slavemaster obliged. He married her under false pretences and got her to sign a slave contract that listed over 100 elements she had to do to please him. Later that year, she too vanished without a trace.

About the same time, nurse Suzette Trouten, gave up her life to travel the world as a submissive sex slave to Robinson. But – you guessed it – she too vanished without a trace.

Letters that were sent to her family after her disappearance were supposed to have come from various foreign countries but instead had the Kansas City postal stamps. It was then the tables started to turn on Robinson. The authorities were catching up to him.

Sex toys to the rescue

Although the internet's first serial killer was becoming known to police, there wasn't enough evidence against him, and without a body or a crime scene, it became impossible to link him to anything. It took a bizarre incident to finally nab him.

In June 2000, an unnamed woman accused him of hitting her and stealing her sex toys. Though the physical attack seemed more serious, the police used the theft of the sex toys as a reason to obtain search warrants for Robinson's property.

A task force was sent to the property expecting to find evidence that Robinson was linked to the disappearances, but what they found, shocked them beyond belief. The team discovered two decomposed bodies within two chemical drums at the back of the building.

They were the remains of Polish immigrant Lewicka, and nurse Trouten. They then searched his storage properties in Missouri, where they discovered three more decomposed corpses in similar looking chemical drums.

The bodies were that of Sheila Faith and her 15-year-old daughter, along with 49-year-old Beverly Bonner, who had been the prison librarian at the same prison where he had been incarcerated. She had never been reported missing.

The five victims had been killed with a powerful blow to the back of the head. The other three missing women have never been found but Robinson pleaded guilty to killing them.

At both sites, there were thousands of photographs of different women in various stages of undress. To this day, investigators have not found any of the women in the photographs. Though some seemed consensual, there were many that didn't.

It remains unclear if he had purchased some of the photos from the so-called International Council of Masters – before the internet, or if they had been taken by himself or others. Some of the locations in the photos have never been identified.

Control

In 2002, after the longest criminal trial in Kansas history, Robinson was found guilty of three murders, and sentenced to death. In Missouri, he pleaded guilty by way of a statement and was convicted of five murders there. For each of the five murders, he received additional life sentences.

Missouri was known at the time to actively pursue death sentences, whereas Kansas was not. By pleading guilty in Missouri, Robinson avoided the death penalty there.

Four years later, in 2006, while Robinson was on death row, the decomposed body of a young woman was found in a chemical barrel in Iowa. Even with DNA testing, the victim has never been identified and may have been inside the barrel for two decades or more.

Investigators later claimed that Robinson's whereabouts for many years were unknown, and he had set up businesses all over the country. But the internet's first serial killer has long remained tight-lipped and silent on the murders and his involvement. Some believe it is the only control he has left.

"He's maintained the secrets about what he's done with the women, he won't ever tell, it's the last control that he's got. There are other barrels waiting to be opened, other bodies

waiting to be found." - an investigator in a 2010 interview with Cold Case Files.

Robinson's case begs the questions; if the International Council of Masters were a real sex cult, then who were the other members and where are they now? Or was it a figment of Robinson's dark imagination?

More importantly, if the photos of the women were not his victims, then who were they and why have they never been identified? It lends to the theory that maybe there are other Slavemaster's out there who have simply evaded capture.

Blood & Fire At Christmas

For survivors of the Covina Massacre, Christmas memories are now filled with blood and fire, and a loss of innocence ripped away by a man dressed as Santa, whose suit melted onto his own skin.

Three years before the Christmas Day Grapevine Massacre, another estranged husband dressed up as Santa and slaughtered his entire family, in what would become known as the Covina Massacre.

Certain crime rates increase around the Christmas period, namely burglaries and murder. Burglaries are intruder-based, and generally not people who are known to the victims. Murders, on the other hand, are mostly known to the victims.

As the Grapevine Massacre and Covina Massacre show, there's no telling the lengths that some people will go to seek revenge on their former loved ones. If Grapevine was bizarre enough due to its location and Santa killer, then Covina was on a whole different level.

On Christmas Eve 2008, in Covina, Los Angeles, 45-year-old Bruce Jeffrey Pardo, dressed up as Santa and drove to his ex-wife's parent's house. He opened fire on around 25 partygoers before setting the property alight with a home-made flamethrower, killing nine people.

Due to the intensity of the fire, the bodies were so badly burned the victims were listed as missing before they could be identified through medical records. Bruce drove to his brother's house and shot himself dead.

When he was found, parts of the Santa suit had melted in the fire and was stuck to his skin. The rest of the suit was found in his car. As part of an elaborate booby-trap, if someone moved the suit, the vehicle was rigged to explode.

Darkness descends

In 2006, electrical engineer Bruce, married the love of his life, Sylvia Ortega, but from that point, their relationship began to deteriorate. Bruce refused to open a joint bank account which led to tensions between them.

Following on from that, Sylvia found out that Bruce had been married previously and was concealing children he had from that relationship. One of the children had been severely injured in a swimming pool accident many years earlier, and Sylvia began to lose trust in her new husband.

Sylvia had three children from a previous marriage and Bruce expected her to take care of her own children with her own finances. He didn't want to financially support her direct family in any way. So, it wasn't too long before Sylvia started looking for a way out.

Not long after their wedding, Sylvia filed for divorce. In June 2008, a divorce court ordered Bruce to pay almost $2,000 (USD) per month in spousal and child support, along with a $10,000 (USD) settlement as part of the divorce.

Bruce countered by saying that Sylvia was rinsing him of everything he owned out of spite. He claimed she would eat out at the most expensive restaurants, bought a luxury car, and took multiple holidays. The court passed the judgement, nonetheless.

A month later, unable to afford the payments to his ex-wife, Bruce falsified his work hours to get more money but was found out and fired from his job. His woes were compacted when he learned that Sylvia was to keep his dog.

Despite having no criminal record and no signs of being violent towards anyone in his life, Bruce finally snapped, and as Christmas approached, he took matters into his own hands.

Rampage

On Christmas Eve 2008, Sylvia's parents, Alicia and Joseph Ortega, were holding a Christmas party at their home in Covina. Sylvia and her children were in attendance, along with her sisters, Leticia, and Alicia, and her brothers, James and Charles, and their families.

Christmas was a time when all the relatives came together in peace and in celebration of the holidays. Later that night, at around 11.30pm, while the party was in full swing, and the family were playing poker, the doorbell rang – an ominous tone that signalled the start of something horrific.

The door was opened and Santa Claus was standing in the doorway with a large, gift-wrapped package under his arm. Upon seeing Santa standing at the entrance of the house, eight-year-old Katrina Yuzefpolsky ran towards him with arms outstretched, welcoming Santa to the party.

Immediately, Bruce pulled out one of the four 9mm handguns he had hidden inside the suit and shot her in the face. He then opened fire at random, shooting people as they tried to escape or hide. As some lay dying, he stood over them and shot them in the head.

That package under his arm was no ordinary Christmas present. Bruce had designed a home-made flamethrower out of a rolling air compressor which had been retrofitted to dispel gasoline. After emptying the guns of all bullets, he used the flamethrower and torched the property from the inside.

Shortly after 11.30pm, emergency services received a call from the Ortega's neighbour. When police arrived on the scene, they had no idea what had happened, as the house was an inferno, with flames as high as fifty feet scorching the Christmas skyline.

Even as the building burned, police were still getting reports of gunfire inside the building, but Bruce had long gone. In fact, he had planned to elope to Mexico but changed his mind at the last minute. At least, that was the speculation.

Endgame

As the inferno was being fought by 80 firefighters, Bruce was on his way to his brother's home, 30 miles away. While using the flamethrower, Bruce had received third-degree burns to his arms and upper body. The flames burned through the flammable Santa outfit and melted parts of it onto his skin.

He managed to get most of it off before entering his brother's home, who wasn't there when Bruce arrived. He placed the rest of the Santa suit on the back seat of his car, with an explosive device that would explode if the suit was lifted.

Three days before the massacre, Bruce had phoned a friend in Illinois to state that he would be headed there over Christmas to join in the celebrations. An airline ticket from Los Angeles to Illinois was later found in Bruce's residence.

Investigators suspected the Illinois visit would have been an attempt to trick them into believing he had gone to Illinois, when he could have been making his way down to Mexico. Inside his later abandoned car were road maps for the United

States and Mexico, along with a computer, clothes, water, and food.

None of the Illinois or Mexico plan was followed through, because in the early hours of Christmas Day, Bruce shot himself dead in his brother's house. As the fire was slowly being brought under control, and police were finding bodies in the ashes, Bruce's brother, Brad, returned home to find Bruce dead on his sofa.

Brad phoned police, who then managed to put two and two together. When police arrived at Brad's home, they found Bruce's body, and sent other officers to find his car. It was parked one block away, and in it, they found an arsenal of weapons. Believing the car to be a threat, police called in the bomb squad.

Triple threat

While the bomb squad were sending in a remote-controlled robot to check the vehicle, police were investigating Bruce's suicide. That's when they found something unusual – which led them to suspect there may have been a second gunman.

Wrapped around Bruce's legs was $17,000 (USD) in cash, which meant he had planned to elope immediately after. They found four empty 9mm handguns and 200 rounds of ammunition. One of the guns was in Bruce's lap, and the other was beside him on the floor.

As police investigated, they found a bullet hole in the ceiling which was unusual as Bruce had shot himself in the side of the head. When another team broke into Bruce's residence on the other side of the city, they found empty boxes for five 9mm handguns, one more than the four Bruce had.

With that, they recovered a tactical shotgun, more ammunition, and enough explosive material to wipe out an entire block of buildings. As the bomb squad robot moved the Santa suit in the back of the car, it caused a small explosion, destroying both the suit and vehicle.

At the burned down Ortega's house, investigators recovered nine bodies. Three had been killed outright with a gun, four died from a combination of gunshot wounds and fire, and two others were from the fire alone. Many of the bodies had to be identified through dental records.

Memories of blood and fire

By Christmas afternoon, police were still unsure if there had been a second shooter. Surviving sibling, Leticia, was interviewed by police and said that the

Santa suit was professional but she identified the person in the suit as Bruce. It remains unclear if she knew by that point that Bruce had killed himself.

Ortega's neighbours identified Bruce's car as the one parked nearby at the time of the fire. Thus the evidence was strongly pointing towards Bruce as the killer. But the issue of the cash, the bullet hole in the ceiling, and the abandoned plan to elope was troubling the investigation.

It seems likely that Bruce was so badly burned by the fire and the melting of the suit that he abandoned the plan and decided to take his own life. The bullet hole in the ceiling, could have been a first attempt at suicide, that he couldn't go through with.

Other debunked theories are that Bruce was not the person in the Santa suit but who it could have been is anyone's guess. Another suggests that upon seeing what Bruce had done, Brad shot his own brother and made it look like a suicide. Again, unlikely, but a theory that is out there, nonetheless.

It was suspected that he had also planned to kill Sylvia's divorce lawyer and had planned to go there after killing the Ortega's but due to the severity of the burns on his body, he drove to his brother's home instead. The car was abandoned just 500 feet from the lawyers house, close to where Brad lived.

Sylvia was shot dead, as was Alicia senior, and Joseph. The other victims were Charles, Cheri, James, Teresa, Alicia, and Michael. 13 children were orphaned during that fateful Christmas massacre. It's a horrific tale of a man pushed to the edge of his own sanity, changing Christmas forever.

And yet, there is a silver-lining to the story, as slim as it may be. Eight-year-old Katrina Yuzefpolsky, who was shot in the face as she ran towards Santa, went on to survive the attack, albeit with lifechanging injuries.

For Katrina, and survivors of the massacre, Christmas memories are now filled with blood and fire, and a loss of innocence ripped away by a man seeking revenge on the world around him. Christmas in Covina has never been the same again.

Killer in the Navy

A gay Petty Officer in the Royal Navy killed at least two young sailors and has since been suspected of killing up to twenty, in one of Hampshire's worst cases of serial killing.

With 1.9million residents, Hampshire is one of the most densely packed counties in England, with only Kent, West Yorkshire, Greater Manchester, West Midlands, and Greater London topping it out. As such, the county has been home to some of the most brutal crimes.

Perhaps no more so than the case of Allan Michael Grimson, whose name has mostly remained protected from international scrutiny, until now. Though convicted of two murders, it has long been suspected that Grimson killed more, with as many as 20 undiscovered victims.

It wasn't only Hampshire that bore the brunt of his violent campaign, he has been linked to murders as far afield as Gibraltar and New Zealand. Despite being a serial killer, Grimson is believed to be held in an open prison, where he is considered low-risk.

Grimson was a sailor with the Royal Navy and travelled to the far corners of the earth with the service, it was this supposed international anonymity that allowed him to claim the victims of his choosing. He was also known as the '*Frankenstein Killer*', who cut off the ears of his victims and slit their throats with a knife.

Born in 1958, in North Shields, Northumberland, Grimson dreamed of joining the Navy and as soon as he was old enough, escaped his hometown and enlisted in 1978. Though the two convicted murders took place in the late nineties, he has long been linked to an unexplained disappearance in 1986.

Grimson was serving on the HMS Illustrious, a light aircraft carrier, while it was docked in Gibraltar. Serving with him on the ship at the time was 18-year-old leading seaman Simon Parkes, born in 1968 in Kingswood, Gloucestershire.

In December 1986, the crew of the Illustrious were afforded some welcome shore leave, after having near circumnavigated the world on a tour known as '*Global 86*'. Gibraltar was the last stop before heading back to the ship's home port in Portsmouth, Hampshire.

On 12th December, Parkes was out drinking with shipmates at a pub called the Horseshoe Bar, when he left to find some food, stating he had drunk a little too much. He was seen in another pub nearby shortly after by a witness who claimed he was so drunk he couldn't stand.

When he didn't return to the ship the following morning, he was assumed missing, and a 250-man search team began scouring the areas he had last been seen but no trace of him was found.

At the time, Parkes was considered to have gone AWOL (absent without leave), but there was no basis for him doing so. He had left his passport in his cabin, along with Christmas presents for his family in England, and a special pass for his family to join him dockside when the Illustrious arrived home.

His shipmates confirmed to their superiors and investigators that Parkes was looking forward to returning home and was not the type to have eloped. It wouldn't be until 2001 when Grimson was linked to his disappearance.

After his convictions, it emerged that Grimson was in the Horseshoe Bar and had been seen drinking with Parkes. Grimson was gay, but not openly so, though he was often seen fraternising with other gay men aboard the ship, especially those younger than him.

In 2003, British police flew to Gibraltar and used specialist teams to search the areas where Parkes was last seen, including local cemeteries. In 2005, the BBC aired two investigative programmes looking into Parkes's disappearance, but in both cases, no body was found.

Both the police and the BBC pointed the finger at Grimson, who was then in jail for the two known murders but they couldn't prove he had killed Parkes. In 2019, Hampshire police received an anonymous tip that Parkes was buried in Trafalgar Cemetery in Gibraltar but it was proven to be false.

The disappearance of Parkes, and Grimson's possible involvement has long been suspected to be true, even more so when we look at a surprising link between Parkes and the murders in the next section, one that would have some researchers reaching for their tin foil hats.

In November 1997, Grimson was on a Navy-run fire-fighting course in Portsmouth when he met 18-year-old fellow sailor Nicholas Wright. He took a fancy to the eager youngster and invited him out for drinks in Portsmouth on a regular basis.

By that point, Grimson had achieved the rank of Petty Officer (PO) but used his ever-increasing power to his advantage. He told Wright that he would drive him back to his home in Leicester on the weekends, and Wright didn't refuse, as it meant a free ride home.

Even at that time, Wright's family were suspicious of Grimson's motives, suspecting he wanted more than a friendship with Wright. On 12th December 1997, Wright and Grimson were drinking together in a Portsmouth nightclub and were seen leaving together in the early hours.

Grimson took Wright back to his flat in London Road, North End, where he attempted to kiss him but Wright pushed him away. Grimson took offence at being refused his sexual advances and started punching Wright in the head. Not willing to let his anger die down, he reached for a nearby baseball bat.

He beat Wright into unconsciousness then cut his throat with a kitchen knife. Bizarrely, he sliced off Wright's ear before placing the body in the bathtub and going to bed. He wanted to take body parts for trophies but decided against it.

The next night, Grimson wrapped Wright's body in black bin bags, put him in the boot of his car and drove towards Cheriton village, 20 miles away. Along the way, while dressed in his Navy uniform, he pulled over to talk to a police officer, knowing that Wright was in the back.

The officer had no idea about the body in the boot of the car and Grimson drove on to Cheriton where he buried Wright's body in a shallow grave on a grassy patch beside the A272 road. The body wouldn't be found until one year later.

Grimson was questioned about the disappearance by police and military police but lied his way out of trouble. He later claimed he got a thrill of putting himself in the firing line and said that *'murder was better than sex'*. He referred to the murder as *'the Nicholas Wright experience'*.

The thrill of the kill had spurred Grimson on to his second confirmed victim, 20-year-old Sion Jenkins, a year later in December 1998. Originally from Newbury, Jenkins had joined the Navy at a young age but decided it wasn't for him and left when he was 19.

Grimson already had his sights set on Jenkins and would frequent the Hogs Head bar in Portsmouth where Jenkins worked after leaving the Navy. On the night of 12th December, Grimson went to

Joanna's Nightclub in Portsmouth and met up with Jenkins.

He lured the drunk barman back to his flat where he forced him to perform sexual acts. After punching and threatening him, he raped Jenkins and tied him to the bed. In the morning, Jenkins begged Grimson to let him leave but Grimson had other ideas.

He wanted to repeat the thrill of the Wright murder and decided to kill Jenkins. He reached for the baseball bat and beat Jenkins until he was no longer breathing, crushing his skull in the process. The following night, he dumped the body on a small area of land on the A32 in West Tisted, 24 miles away, and only four miles from where he had buried Wright.

When police investigated the disappearance, Grimson's name kept coming up in witness statements as someone who might have been involved. In late December 1998, 40-year-old Grimson was brought into Portsmouth Police station for an interview, where he confessed to Wright's murder.

Grimson told police where they could find Wright's body. Then, feeling the power afforded to him by his actions, Grimson confessed to

Jenkins's murder, which was only considered to be a disappearance at the time.

A day after digging up Wright's body, police were led to where Jenkins had been buried. Grimson was charged with both murders and ultimately went to trial, when in 2001 he was convicted of both and sentenced to 22 years in prison.

The sentence was increased to 25 years by the then Home Secretary, with a side note that he should never be released. Yet, in 2008, his sentence was reduced by three years on appeal, based on his guilty plea, time spent on remand, and a psychological report revealing an undiagnosed personality disorder.

A specialised psychiatrist who had amassed decades of research and had studied 250 other murderers and serial killers, met with Grimson, and later told the media that he was the worst psychopath he had ever come across.

The judge at the trial told Grimson, *'you are a serial killer in nature if not in number. You are a highly dangerous serial killer who killed two young men in horrifying circumstances.'* It was around the time of Grimson's conviction that police began looking into other murders.

The FBI's definition of a serial killer is the unlawful killing of two or more victims by the same offender in separate events. Britain doesn't have a standard and either tends to use the FBI definition, or three, depending on the police force. This researcher suggests three is the definition within Britain.

And as such, when investigators began looking closer at Grimson's movements, they discovered an eerie link between the two confirmed victims. Both had been killed on 12th December, one year apart. With that in mind, they began to link up Grimson's movements on the same date for every year he was in the Navy.

The 12th of December link was the sole reason Grimson was linked to the Parkes disappearance in Gibraltar. In an unusual twist of fate, Parkes had also gone missing on 12th December and was presumed dead or killed.

With the date theory in place, it was suggested by police that Grimson may have been deliberately killing people on the 12th of December every year since 1978, which meant there could have been at least 20 victims.

It was the date theory that led to the police and the BBC investigating the Parkes disappearance in 2003 and 2005 respectively. When they began tracking Grimson's movements, a team of specialist British detectives landed in New Zealand to look through missing persons reports and unsolved murder files.

Grimson had been in Auckland as a Royal Navy fire instructor for four months between June and September 1998. One unsolved murder matched the dates. 29-year-old Japanese student Kayo Matsuzawa was found locked inside a fire alarm cabinet near to where Grimson was teaching, 11 days after she disappeared.

Though a different victim profile and not part of the date theory, the murder was linked to Grimson. It was suspected Kayo was drugged, stripped, and left naked in the airtight cabinet where she suffocated to death. The building manager, who was friendly with Grimson, had seen him in the building on the date of Kayo's disappearance.

Grimson has long since denied connections with other murders or the date theory but investigators still believe he may be responsible for up to 20 murders in total. When some of his interviews were made public, it emerged that Grimson fitted the profile of a thrill killer.

In one interview, he said he used the fire-instructor course to select his victims, from the ranks of trainees and cadets. He would zone-in on the one he enjoyed looking at the most and pass them through to the next stage of training quicker than the rest.

The higher level training was more personal and he was able to dominate and select the best looking trainees for his own pleasure. Then he would scour the local nightclubs looking for them or other men to satisfy his sexual desire.

In 2019, Grimson became eligible for parole and was transferred to an open prison. In Britain, an open prison is a jail in which prisoners are trusted to complete their sentences with minimal supervision. It is generally for prisoners who are considered low-risk to gradually help them reintegrate into society.

For the families of the victims, missing and dead, Grimson's transfer to an open prison was a hammer blow, made worse by the fact the state considered him to be low risk. Whether a serial killer or not, Grimson left a dark stain on the British Navy, one that continues to haunt to this day.

The Scream Killers

Inspired by the movie 'Scream', two teenagers hide out in their friend's basement, to scare and kill their victim – while making their own macabre documentary about it.

Pre-meditated murder or murder in the first degree is a charge given to those who intentionally plan to murder another human being. In the case of 16-year-olds Brian Lee Draper and Torey Michael Adamcik, the charge of first-degree murder could never have been more apt.

Their love of scary movies, specifically the Scream franchise, led them to a friend's house on 22nd September 2006, in the sleepy American city of Pocatello, Idaho. There, they would brutally murder schoolmate and friend, 16-year-old Cassie Jo Stoddart.

What makes this case so bizarre, is not just the detailed planning and shocking aspect of it, but the fact they recorded themselves talking about the murder, before, during, and afterwards.

On the day of the murder, they even approached Cassie at school while she was opening her locker. They shoved a video camera in her face and stated her name before asking her to say hi to the camera. Before that moment, they had already planned to kill her and her friends.

They wanted to kill Cassie for one simple reason – fame.

Day before the murder

Cassie was well known and liked in the school where she studied and it wasn't hard to find out where she would be at any particular time. She was due to housesit her aunt and uncle's home on Whispering Cliff's Drive. Allison and Frank Contreras were headed out for the weekend and trusted Cassie with their home.

Before Cassie arrived at the home the following day, her killers had already put their shocking plan into action. But it wasn't only Cassie they wanted to kill, whoever was going to be in the house at the time, would become their victims.

Included in this story are real life transcripts of the videos that Draper and Adamcik recorded. The first was recorded the day before the murder.

Draper: We found our victim and sad as it may be she's our friend but you know what? We all have to make sacrifices. Our first victim is going to be Cassie Stoddart and her friend. We'll let you (*Laughs*) we'll find out if she has friends over, if she's going to be alone in a big dark house out in the middle of nowhere (*Laughs*). How perfect can you get? I, I mean like holy shit dude.

Adamcik: I'm horny just thinking about it.

Draper: Hell yeah. So we're gonna fucking kill her and her friends and we're gonna keep moving on. I heard some news, she's gonna be home alone from six to seven so we might kill her and drive over to Cassie's thing and scare the shit out of them and kill them one by fucking one. Hell yeah.

Adamcik: Why one by one? Why can't it be a slaughterhouse?

Draper: Two by two and three by three. Cause we've got to keep it classy.

Adamcik: Keep it classy.

Draper: So yeah. It's going to be extra fun.

Later in the video:

Draper: We are sick psychopaths who get their pleasure off killing other people.

Adamcik: That sounds good baby.

Draper: We're gonna go down in history. We're gonna be just like Scream except real life terms.

Adamcik: That sounds good baby.

Draper: We're gonna be murderers. Like, let's see, Ted Bundy, like the Hillside Strangler.

Adamcik: No.

Draper: The Zodiac Killer.

Adamcik: Those people were more amateurs compared to what we are going to be.

Draper: Murder is power, murder is freedom, goodbye.

Night of the murder

While housesitting, Cassie got a knock at the door. Her boyfriend, Matt Beckham, showed up to watch a movie with her. As they settled down to watch Kill Bill Volume 2, Draper and Adamcik arrived to hang out and sit with them.

They asked Cassie to give them a tour of the residence and she obliged, they were particular interested in the basement. A short while later, Draper and Adamcik told Cassie and Matt they were going to go to a cinema instead.

As far as Cassie and Matt were aware, the two guys went to the cinema. The truth was vastly different. On their way out, Draper and Adamcik had unlocked the basement door and the back door, so they could re-enter the residence undetected.

Draper and Adamcik waited in a car near the house.

Draper: The time is 9:50, September 22nd, 2006. Um ... unfortunately we have the gruelling task of killing our two friends and they are right in—in that house just down the street.

Adamcik: We just talked to them. We were there for an hour, but ...

Draper: We checked out the whole house. We know there's lots of doors. There, there's lots of places to hide. Um, I unlocked the back doors. It's all unlocked. Now we just got to wait and um ... yep, we're, we're really nervous right now but, you know, we're ready.

Adamcik: We're listening to the greatest rock band ever.

Draper: We've waited for this for a long time.

Adamcik: Pink Floyd. Before we commit the ultimate crime of murder.

Draper: We've waited for this for a long time.

Adamcik: A long time

Draper: We—well stay tuned.

The murder

Draper and Adamcik crept back into the house and made their way to the basement, where they wanted to carry out the murders. Their first plan was to make some noise to lure Cassie and Matt downstairs.

When that failed, they switched off the electrics to the house with the basement circuit breaker box. They switched them back on shortly after. Cassie noticed the Contreras' dog barking at the basement door and became scared, more so when the lights went on and off again.

Matt called his mother and asked if he could stay over at Cassie's to look after her. His mother refused but offered Cassie to come back with Matt.

Cassie turned the offer down, saying the house was her responsibility and she had to look after it.

At 10:30pm, Matt's mother picked him up from the residence. On the way back, Matt called Adamcik's phone to see if he could hang out. Adamcik answered but whispered quietly, so Matt couldn't hear him properly. Believing Adamcik and Draper to be in the cinema, he didn't give it a second thought.

Draper and Adamcik tried turning off the lights again to lure Cassie into the basement but she remained in the living room. They crept up the basement stairs and slammed a closet door to scare her.

Looking around in the darkness, Cassie could see no-one so she laid back down on the couch to see Draper and Adamcik standing over her. They stabbed her 30 times with hunting knives, killing her instantly and leaving her body in the living room.

As they drove away from the house, their video log continued.

Draper: Just killed Cassie! We just left her house. This is not a fucking joke.

Adamcik: I'm shaking.

Draper: I stabbed her in the throat, and I saw her lifeless body. It just disappeared. Dude, I just killed Cassie!

Adamcik: Oh my God!

Draper: Oh, oh fuck. That felt like it wasn't even real. I mean it went by so fast.

Adamcik: Shut the fuck up. We gotta get our act straight.

Draper: It's okay. Okay? We—we'll just buy movie tickets now.

Aftermath

Two days later, Allison and Frank Contreras returned from their weekend getaway with Cassie's 13-year-old cousin. The cousin found Cassie's body in the living room and screamed, alerting the adults to her discovery.

Matt Beckham was initially a suspect in the murder but led them to Draper and Adamcik who were arrested five days later. Draper and Adamcik both blamed each other and said the other person forced them into doing it.

Until the tapes were found, buried by the pair shortly after the murder.

Draper claimed he was inspired by the Columbine High School Massacre in 1999, while Adamcik cited the Scream movie franchise as his inspiration. Though they were 16-years-old at the time of the murder, both were tried as adults and sentenced to life in prison without the possibility of parole.

They may not ever have realised the damage they left behind. Cassie's aunt lost her job and fell into a deep depression. Cassie's cousin, who had found the body, was known to have attempted suicide on multiple occasions.

When they tried to sell the house to move on from the murder, no offers were put in. Their once dream home had become a nightmare, trapping them in perpetual memory of what had happened there.

Bow Cinema Axeman

During the Golden Age of movies, a cinema attendant took an axe to his manager and eloped with a suitcase full of money, in a tale of premeditated murder, historical horrors, and a fake death.

London was at the heart of the burgeoning cinema business in the 1930s, and the Borough of Tower Hamlets was packed full of them, as business owners realised the opportunity that could be afforded to them.

The areas of Bow and Mile End within Tower Hamlets were once home to no less than 33 cinemas with many of the independent ones no longer active, most destroyed in the Second World War and rebuilt as residential property.

One such cinema was the Bow Palace Cinema, sometimes known as the Eastern Palace Cinema due to its heritage. Originally a pub built in 1855, it became the Eastern Empire Theatre in 1892, before becoming the Palace Theatre from 1899 to 1917.

In 1923, it was redeveloped and became home to the Bow Palace Cinema, though many still referred to it as the Eastern. At the time it was taken over by businessman and movie-lover Dudley Henry Hoard and his wife Maisie – until they were brutally attacked by one of their employees.

John Stockwell

By 1934, the cinema was in full swing, taking advantage of the wave of early British and American movies. 19-year-old John Frederick Stockwell was employed as one of the many cinema attendants that helped usher in the crowds and sell tickets.

But John was suddenly tempted into thievery by the amount of money the cinema was taking. On an average weekend, the cinema was reeling in £100, approximately £7,500 in today's money.

John's father, also named John Stockwell, was killed in the First World War, just months after

John Junior's birth. Growing up without a father during the fallout of the war was hard enough but his mother died when he was a toddler and John was ultimately raised in various orphanages.

He ended up spending a majority of his childhood in the care of the Salvation Army and their homes. At first, when he got the job at the cinema, he was ecstatic. He was able to watch new films as they were released and expand his social circle as he was friendly with the cinema-goers.

Yet, that life of hardship being raised with no family and little to no money was grinding him down. Surely there must be another way to live well? With that in mind, he began noting how much money the cinema was taking, and for want of a better phrase – finally gave into temptation.

The axeman cometh

Over the weekend of 4th to 5th August 1934, John developed his plan and began to look at where the cinema's takings were being collected. Each night, the money was put into a safe and after each weekend was put into a suitcase by the owner Dudley, for transportation to the local bank.

On the morning of Tuesday 7th August 1934, Dudley was about to leave with the suitcase of money after a bumper weekend when there was a knock at the door. He opened it to find John standing outside who immediately pushed the doors open and entered the cinema.

John wasn't supposed to be working that day and Dudley knew right away that something was wrong. When John – who hadn't tried to disguise himself – attempted to remove the suitcase from the building, he got into a fight with Dudley.

Desperately needing the money and believing it to be the start of a better life, John removed a fire axe he had hidden in his long coat, stormed back into the foyer and hit Dudley over the head with the blade end.

As Dudley fell to the ground, John hit Maisie in the head and she collapsed in a heap. Realising Dudley was still alive, John hit him in the head with the axe another thirteen times, fracturing his skull and killing him instantly.

John then made off with the suitcase, believing both of them to be dead. When the cleaners arrived in the late morning, they walked into the scene of a bloodbath. Dudley was lying in a pool of blood with his head split open and Maisie had seemingly suffered the same fate – until she was found to be alive.

Eagle-eyed holidaymakers

Emergency services arrived at the cinema within minutes as no such crime had been so brazenly committed for many years in Bow. Maisie was rushed to hospital where surgeons managed to keep her alive. Unfortunately for Dudley, it was too late, as he had died at the scene.

Police intricately searched the building and discovered a bloody axe behind the curtains on the stage. Along one of the walls they found a bloody fingerprint that belonged to the killer but with no other witnesses, they needed motive.

Maisie regained consciousness shortly after noon and confirmed with police that the motive was robbery. Even though John worked for the cinema, Maisie could not identify her attacker and said he was a boy in his late teens.

It appeared the mysterious axeman had eloped without a trace but John had another plan in place to disappear for good and it would lead to his downfall. Three days after the murder, John travelled to the coastal town of Lowestoft, 125 miles northeast of Bow.

On the morning of 10th August, Lowestoft police received a suicide letter that was found on Lowestoft beach. The letter was signed by John as

J. F. Stockwell and he confessed to Dudley's murder along with the theft.

Though initially not a suspect due to the day of the murder being his day off, John was now prime suspect number one, except it appeared he had taken his own life. When details of the letter were released to the press the same day, some eagle-eyed Lowestoft holidaymakers reported an unusual sight.

Victim of his own stupidity

The same morning the note had been received, various holidaymakers saw a young man place a pile of neatly folded clothes on the golden sandy shoreline, despite already wearing clothes. Nothing was thought of it, until the confession letter was heard of on the news.

Police were directed to the pile of clothes the same afternoon, where they found items belonging to John, in addition to his watch and Post Office savings book – with his name on it. It appeared John's plan was to trick the police into believing he had taken his own life by walking into the sea.

He probably didn't expect that Lowestoft holidaymakers were as eagle-eyed as those elsewhere. When police found out that John had walked away from the beach and not into the sea, a nationwide manhunt went into effect.

The next day on the 14th, John checked into the Metropolitan Hotel in Great Yarmouth, ten miles up the coast. He gave a fake name and his address as Luton, Hertfordshire. When John went up to his room, the hotel manager became suspicious as there was no Luton in Hertfordshire, it was in fact in Bedfordshire.

The hotel had already received word of the manhunt of a young man who may have been in and around Great Yarmouth. The hotel manager believed that John fitted the description of the killer, and combined with the address mistake, called in the police.

Death sentence

When John walked out of the hotel just minutes later, the manager thought he may have spooked him but it turned out that John wanted to go on a shopping spree. Police were made aware of his location and they watched him enter many shops, stocking up on pricey goods.

When John arrived back at the hotel, Great Yarmouth police were waiting for him and arrested him on sight. Knowing the game was up, John didn't resist arrest. He was interviewed in Great Yarmouth where he confessed and was driven back down to London to face charges.

Two months later on 22nd October, after a very public trial, John pleaded guilty to murder but he had a story already laid out. When John had arrived at the cinema that fateful morning, he claimed that he told Dudley he'd left personal money in the building and was going to retrieve it.

He believed his personal money was in the suitcase of cash and when he tried to look inside, Dudley stopped him, resulting in an axe to the head. Yep, the court didn't believe him either and he was ultimately convicted of murder.

The fact that John had taken an axe to the cinema in the first instance and planned his fake death meant it was a pre-meditated murder, and as such received the harshest sentence – death.

Horrors of the past

On 14th November 1934, John was led to the gallows at Pentonville Prison and had no final words to say. He was executed by hanging that same morning. A total of 120 men between 1902 and 1961 were executed at Pentonville Prison, and it remains one of Britain's most notorious execution sites.

For Maisie, justice had been served, and though she didn't make a full recovery from her injuries, she lived out the rest of her life as best she could. Her husband, Dudley, had been buried three days after John was captured.

Due to the tragedy that had befallen the cinema, it was rebuilt as an Art Deco style building to become the Regal Cinema. As fate would have it, the building was bombed by Germans during the Second World War.

The Regal was rebuilt again and reopened in 1947 before ultimately closing its doors for good in 1958. Built upon the ruins of bombings and bloody murder, the site has been home to various residential buildings, with many tenants unaware of the horrors of the past.

Horror Movie Killer

A man inspired by horror movies went on a rampage that left four dead and two injured, in a tragic case that laid the blame at the feet of those put in place to protect the public.

Though many horror movies are said to incite violence, they are no less inciting than watching a 24-hour news cycle. Many violent people who it is said were influenced by horror movies already have something wrong within them that causes them to lash out, and none more so than in the case of David Gonzalez.

Between the 15th and 17th September 2004, David, aged 24, went on a killing spree wearing a hockey mask similar to the one Jason Vorhees wears in the Friday the 13th films. Though wearing a hockey mask, he later claimed that he was similar to Freddy Krueger from Nightmare on Elm Street.

The killing spree was a result of the failure of the system to protect David from himself and others, something that will become evidently clear shortly. David stocked up on various drugs, took a knife from his mother's kitchen and walked out the house intent on killing.

So intent on killing that he was aiming to become the most notorious serial killer in history. He wrote about his experiences in letter form calling himself Zippy. When he was committed to the maximum security Broadmoor psychiatric hospital, the doctors said he was the sickest patient they had ever seen and that the killing spree could have been prevented.

Born in 1980 in Surrey to an English mother, Lesley, and Spanish father, he was raised in a good household and educated at a private school in Woking. His parents split up when he was six, and his mother remarried his stepfather Steven Harper shortly after.

He left school with good grades and was known to be an expert at chess but from the age of 17, David required mental health care. For reasons unknown, he was found to be a troubled teenager who had severe psychological problems.

By the age of 24, he was unable to find work and was using drugs. He spent most of his time playing video games and watching horror movies. There were a number of unusual incidents before his killing spree where he required professional help but was never given it.

During his late teens and early twenties, his mother, Lesley, contacted authorities on multiple occasions but was told each time that a crisis would have to occur before David could get the help he needed.

She even wrote a letter to her MP and social services asking why her son would have to commit a serious offence before being taken seriously. In the letter, she said, *'does David have to murder someone before he can get the treatment he so badly needs?'* Neither the MP nor social services replied.

In 2003, a year before the murders, David himself wrote a letter to his GP that said he needed help and was trying to cope with life as a normal human being but unable to succeed in doing so.

In the letter, regarding previous mental health help he had received in 1998 when he was 18, he wrote, *'I really need to go to hospital voluntarily and receive treatment under the care of the doctors before my mental state gets worse.'*

The letter continued, *'please, please help me, this is very urgent. I really would appreciate if you would help me improve as I am in a desperate situation.'* And despite his doctor making an appointment with him, David was never admitted to hospital.

After the murders, Lesley said she knew something bad was going to happen but everywhere she turned, her calls for help were turned down. The day before the killing spree, Steven was sitting in a car outside the family home when David ran out the front door naked.

It was around the time that Steven was about to drive to work which meant schoolchildren were on their way to school in their droves. David had run out into the street and was seen naked by many children. Steven drove after him but lost him in the streets around their home.

He phoned Lesley at her job and told her that David was running around town naked. She told him to go home and wait for him but David was already there when he got back. He was standing naked in the front room and answered Steven in a deep growly voice.

Steven then did the only thing he could have done in that situation – phoned the police. On the phone he mentioned that David may be suffering from paranoid schizophrenia and was not taking any medication for it as he hadn't been diagnosed yet.

While he was on the phone, David began punching himself in the head, giving himself a black eye. He later said that he wanted to hurt himself as much as possible, to degrade his body and harm his flesh. He even threw himself down the stairs three times to break his bones.

Despite exposing himself in public, calls from a worried stepfather, clear instances of self-harm, the police never came, and three days later, four people would be dead because of it.

The next day, Wednesday 15th September 2004, David jumped on a train to Portsmouth and departed the train at Portsmouth and Southsea station. He walked the short distance to Hilsea where he saw an elderly couple out with their dog.

He approached 61-year-old Peter King and his wife and told them in no uncertain terms that he was going to kill them. David pulled the knife from his pocket and attacked the couple but Peter managed to fight him off, and David ran away from the scene. Peter and his wife were the lucky ones.

David caught a train to Southwick, a few miles east of Brighton, where he departed the train and went on the hunt for another victim. As he went on the hunt, he put on a hockey mask like Jason Vorhees, and found 73-year-old Marie Harding walking alone on a footpath.

He approached her from behind and stabbed her in the back before cutting her throat and running off with her purse. Police spent the next 48 hours searching the area around the crime scene and looking for any witnesses of which there were none. The hockey mask was found nearby and later tested positive for David's DNA.

Unknown to police, David had caught a train back up to London and went back home with no-one questioning where he had been. A day later and with no sign of the law closing in, he went on the lookout for his next victims, in an attempt to become one of the worst serial killers in the history of Britain.

At 5am on Friday 17th September, he caught a train to Tottenham, North London. There, on Tottenham High Road, David walked up behind 46-year-old Kevin Molloy and stabbed him in the face with knives he had stolen from a department store the day before. When Kevin retaliated, David stabbed him in the chest and neck, killing him instantly.

Less than two hours later in nearby Hornsby, 59-year-old Koumis Constantinou was lying in bed when he awoke to find David standing over him.

Koumis was stabbed many times before his wife walked back into the room and managed to fight David off, who then ran out the house.

Fortunately, Koumis survived the attack but was left with life-changing injuries. Less than 15 minutes later, David broke into the home of Derek and Jean Robinson in Highgate. They were just waking up for the day when David stabbed them both in the throat, killing them instantly.

After receiving multiple reports of a madman on the loose, police descended on the area around Tottenham and ultimately arrested David at Tottenham Court Road Tube station, where he was seen by commuters covered in blood. He had also been spotted by a painter and decorator leaving the Robinson's home with a knife.

During the attacks, David had taken lots of drugs, which he claimed made the murders feel *'orgasmic.'* It was already clear that if he wasn't arrested he would have gone on to kill as many as he could. During the trial and found in subsequent letters written by him he claimed the murders to have been *'one of the best things I've done in my life.'*

In each of the letters he referred to himself as Zippy, which was a nickname he'd had since childhood for unknown reasons. He also claimed that he wanted to get professional help before the murders but no-one would help him. If they had then he said the murders would never have happened.

At the trial it materialised that he was inspired to kill by some of his favourite horror characters, most notably Freddy Krueger and Jason Vorhees. Although he had worn the Jason Vorhees mask when he killed Marie Harding, he likened himself to Freddy Krueger and would sometimes tape knives to his fingers and pretend to be the character.

Before his trial, David was kept at the maximum security Broadmoor psychiatric hospital. While there, he attempted to bite through an artery in his arm, in an incident so severe that doctors said they had never seen someone bite themselves with such ferocity.

And then, despite his obvious mental health condition and danger to himself, his plea of guilty by diminished responsibility was rejected. The prosecution made him out to be a calculating psychopath who killed because he was the epitome of evil.

In 2006, in another failure by the system, a jury agreed that David was not mentally ill and found him guilty of four murders as a normal human being. He was handed down six life sentences, four for murder and two for violent assault.

And yet, despite the courts finding him to be a capable and culpable criminal, David was still imprisoned at Broadmoor. There, the doctors attempting to treat him said that he was the most disturbed patient they had ever seen.

Just one year later, in 2007, after another attempt at biting himself to death, David slashed his wrists with parts of a broken CD case and died of massive blood loss. His suicide in a maximum security hospital raised even further questions about he had been treated and not treated.

It's no surprise that after David's suicide, an inquiry was held, which found the Surrey and Borders NHS Foundation Trust lacking in their support of someone with severe mental health issues.

The trust apologised to David's victims and their families and implemented new recommendations and regulations when it came to treating mental health patients both before and after a family member reports that they need help.

But for the families of the dead and injured, the inquiry had come too late, and their lives were forever altered by a man believing himself to be Freddy Krueger, someone who with the right help could have got the treatment he needed to have never committed murder.

Satanic Murder in a Church

A young newlywed went to church to pray and fell victim to an evil killer who did unspeakable things to her body. The killer got away with it for almost half a century until he was finally revealed.

Everyone was against Satanism in the Seventies and Eighties, none more so than the newspapers, who had instilled the notion of Satanic Panic. The fear of Satanism, and occultism to some degree, was only bolstered by the occasional murder that appeared to be ritualistic.

Perhaps no more so than the ritualistic murder of 19-year-old Arlis Perry on 12th October 1974 in California. Fortunately for Arlis, unlike many other murders of the era, a cold case investigation was able to solve it after 44 years.

At the time, the case was linked to Satanists, cults, gangs, serial killers, and the Son of Sam murderer; David Berkowitz, who expressed that he knew more about the murder than the police themselves.

For almost half a century, Arlis' case was one of the most infamous in relation to possible Satanic ritual, and when you read on how she had come to meet her fate, you might just realise why. For her death and desecration of her body was nothing if not born out of absolute evil.

Evil was afoot

Born Arlis Kay Dykema in Bismarck, North Dakota, she was raised in a deeply religious family, and carried on the religious trend throughout her teenage years. The love of her life was Bruce D. Perry, and they had been infatuated with each other since high school.

In August 1974, six weeks before her death, the high school sweethearts married at a small ceremony in North Dakota. Bruce, who was a sophomore pre-med student, was going to study in California, and the couple moved there within days of being married.

They moved into Quillen Hall on the Stanford University campus, and Arlis managed to find work as a receptionist at a local law firm. With a new job, and a new marriage, the couple had already started planning for their future. But evil was afoot in the grounds of Stanford University.

Just before midnight on 12th October, the young couple argued over the tyre pressure on their car. Feeling stressed about the situation, Arlis wanted to go and pray alone at the Stanford Memorial Church, which was an iconic landmark on the University campus.

At around 3am, Bruce became worried that Arlis hadn't returned home, and called the police. Shortly after, officers went to the church to check on Arlis but found the doors to the building were locked, and there were no signs of life inside.

One of the campus security guards, and former police officer, Stephen Black Crawford, said he locked the church at around midnight, the time when Arlis had supposedly gone there. He also did a check of the church at 2am, as was common with the nightshift routine.

When Crawford went to the church at 5.45am to open it for the early morning mass, he stumbled upon Arlis' body.

Ritualistic murder

In the east transept of the cross-shaped church, and near the altar, was the partially nude body of

Arlis. She was lying on her back with her face turned up to the roof. Embedded in the back of her head was an ice pick, which had been broken off from the handle, due to the force of the attack.

A one-metre tall altar candle had been forcibly pushed into her vagina, and another same-sized candle was rested in-between her breasts. Her jeans had been arranged on her legs in a diamond shape pattern. She also had neck injuries consistent with violent strangulation.

Crawford said he had found the west side door open and it had been forced from the inside, which led investigators to suspect the killer or killers were inside the church when Crawford was performing his early morning checks of the perimeter.

Immediately, both Bruce and Crawford became suspects. Investigators found semen on a pillow next to Arlis' body, and a partial palm print on one of the candles. Both pieces of evidence didn't match the pair, and they were removed from the suspect list.

Detectives at the time initially linked the bizarre murder to three previous ones in the same area, that had occurred in the previous year. Those murders were later attributed to American serial killer John Arthur Getreu, who was arrested in 2018 and sentenced to life in prison.

But for a while, the Arlis murder had everyone stumped. The ritualistic style of her death led some officers to consider that Satanic groups were involved, even though there is no known ritual in occultism or elsewhere involving the insertion of a candle into a vagina.

Son of Sam

Detectives discovered that seven people had been in the church on the 12th of October, including Bruce and Crawford, who along with four others were ruled out. A seventh person remained unidentified but a passing witness came forward to claim that he saw a man trying to enter the church around midnight.

The witness said the man had sandy-coloured hair, was of medium build, and was not wearing a watch, which was a bizarre thing to notice. Despite the brutal nature of the murder and display of the body, the Arlis case went cold.

Five years later, serial killer David Berkowitz, AKA: The Son of Sam, wrote about the Arlis murder in a number of letters which were picked up the San Jose Mercury News team. In it, he claimed that the alleged culprit of the Arlis murder was someone he referred to as 'Manson II'.

Investigative journalist, Maury Terry, had become convinced that David Berkowitz, who killed six people and injured nine, did not act alone. The theory goes that Berkowitz was part of a Satanic cult involving at least three other members, and that Manson II was a codename for one of the individuals in that group.

One theory rested on the belief that Arlis was aware of a cult in the area and had gone to the church that night, in an attempt to convert them back to Christianity and its values. But the investigation could find no link between Satanism or Berkowitz.

As the years went by, a retired Santa Clara Police detective, Ken Kahn, theorised that Crawford had locked Arlis into the church by mistake, along with another unidentified person. That person then crept up on Arlis and killed her before breaking out through the west side door.

Yet, the ritualistic style of the murder was not lost on researchers down the years. The case went cold until 2018 when advancements in DNA technology and genetic genealogy testing revealed the true identity of the killer, someone who had been hiding in plain sight.

Hiding in plain sight

In 2018, after confirming DNA evidence they had on record, police went to a San Jose apartment with a search and arrest warrant. The apartment belonged to the then 72-year-old security guard, Stephen Crawford.

He had managed to keep police off his scent from just a few hours after the murder and had maintained his secret for almost half a century. When police arrived at the property, Crawford locked himself in, got hold of his gun, and shot himself in the head, dying of his wound immediately.

Police had always suspected Crawford, due to the timescales of when he performed his checks but they needed advancements in DNA technology to prove it. The breakthrough came when Arlis' clothes were retested for DNA, and it matched that of Crawford's.

Crawford had gone into the church when Arlis was praying and stabbed her in the back of the head with the ice pick before doing things to her body that the first officers on the scene would never forget. It was suspected he did so as an opportunistic act but also out of his hatred for the University.

Despite knowing who killed Arlis, the connection to David Berkowitz remains, as in Crawford's apartment were numerous books about the occult and the Son of Sam, leading some researchers to suspect that Crawford was part of the same secret Satanic cult as Berkowitz.

For 88-year-old Jean Dykema, Arlis' mother, she was shocked and yet relieved that her daughter's killer had finally been revealed, despite the killer not facing justice. For Arlis' father, he had passed away only three months before Crawford was identified and went to the grave not knowing who had really killed his daughter.

Whether the Satanic Panic of the Seventies and Eighties was a smokescreen or a legitimate epidemic, it remains clear that many feared it was real. Crawford may have been trying to emulate the darkness that Satanism evoked. Or maybe he was a Berkowitz fanatic who chose to kill when the opportunity presented itself.

As for Arlis, her case was closed almost half a century after her death, bringing hope to all the other families waiting for justice in the annals of historical true crime. Waiting for that same knock on the door to tell them their loved one's killer has finally been found.

A Twist in the Murder Tale

After a body of a woman was found near a motorway, police rushed to her home to find her husband bound and gagged, claiming they were attacked by a man in a clown mask – but a twist this way comes.

Born in 1955 Coventry, Carol Heslop had a passion for ten-pin bowling and went on to become a member of the Coventry bowling league, where she met her future husband, Gordon Wardell in 1979. They married three years later, and Carol took a job as a cashier at the Coventry branch of the Woolwich Building Society, a financial institution bought out by Barclays in 2000.

She was so good at her job that she quickly rose the ranks, and by 1992 was promoted to branch manager at the nearby Nuneaton branch, nine miles north. By that time, the loving couple were living in the village of Meriden, seven miles from Coventry and only 16 from Birmingham.

As far as family and friends could tell, the relationship between Carol and Gordon was moving smoothly and the pair were seen as relatively wealthy. Gordon had climbed the ranks of a car component business to the point where he was an executive manager but he was taking a lot of time off work.

While Carol was out working, Gordon lived a secret lifestyle where he became addicted to using sex workers. He paid £50 each time to various women to have sex with him while he was tied up, something which he had grown to enjoy.

Six months before her murder, 39-year-old Carol had found out about 42-year-old Gordon's fetish for sex workers and refused to have sex with him. It was about the same time that Gordon was fired from his job for reasons that have never been disclosed, probably due to the amount of time he was taking off.

Then, in September 1994, murder found its way to Nuneaton. In the early morning of the 21st, Carol's lifeless body was spotted by a passing motorist at the side of a grassy verge on the A444, a country road in the Nuneaton area. It sparked a murder investigation unlike any seen in the area before.

Robbery

Detectives arrived on the scene quickly and cordoned off the area. Carol had been strangled to death and there had been no attempt to hide the body, her left sandal was found metres away but her right one was missing. It was suspected she was thrown from a moving vehicle.

Half hour later, staff members from the Nuneaton branch of The Woolwich phoned police to report a break-in, and that there was no sign of their boss, Carol, who was the key-owner for the building. Suspecting an armed robbery, the police sent in the big guns.

Armed police arrived at the scene along with a helicopter that remained stationary above the building. They entered the branch and found there was no sign of forced entry, the alarms hadn't gone off, but all the cash from the vault was missing.

The detectives at the murder scene learned from forensic officers that Carol's own security code had been used to access the vault at approximately 5am that morning, and that her own keys were used to unlock the main door.

Just over £14,000 and numerous blank cheques were missing from the vault. This, along with Carol's body led detectives to the logical conclusion that Carol had been kidnapped and used by armed robbers to access the vault, before being murdered and dumped on the side of the road.

But by that point, no one had heard from Gordon Wardell. There might have been a slim possibility that the armed robbers were in the Wardell's property holding Gordon hostage, so armed police and the detectives descended on the home.

Police forced their way into the property, expecting to find either a dead body or resistance from armed robbers. Instead, what met them was an unusual sight. Gordon was found in his underwear, gagged, and tied to a chair in the middle of the front room.

A clown mask

His clothes were folded neatly beside him, and he appeared to be in a state of distress. He had been gagged with a strip of cloth and tied to a refuse sack holder with two ratchet ties around his wrists. Despite being conscious and alert, he was found with bruising on his stomach and chest.

Paramedics arrived on the scene but didn't have to do much as Gordon's bruises were superficial and didn't require care, they also noted that his blood pressure and heartbeat were low, which would have been odd considering the ordeal that Gordon claimed he went through.

He stated that he arrived home from the pub at 10pm the night before, to find a man wearing a clown mask and boiler suit and holding his wife at knifepoint on the living room sofa. Two other men grabbed him from behind and used some kind of chemical to knock him out for at least ten hours.

Gordon became conscious at around 6am but couldn't escape from his restraints to alert police, which they found unusual as the ratchet ties around his wrists were noted as being *'loose enough to have escaped from with ease, should one have wanted to.'*

For a little while longer, detectives believed his story but the following day, while he was being interviewed by them, his story began to break down. It appeared that there might not have been a kidnapping at all and that Gordon was behind the robbery and his wife's murder.

Previous attack

Despite their suspicions, detectives decided to hold a press conference, not least as it was part of the murder process when a suspect had not been arrested, but also to see how Gordon would cope with different questions being put to him.

Regardless of his superficial wounds, Gordon appeared at the press conference in a wheelchair, wearing sunglasses, and acting nervously around people. Through tears, he told the same story to the press, that a man in a clown mask held his wife at knifepoint, before he was rendered unconscious by two other men.

He then claimed not to have remembered anything else until he awoke later bound and gagged in the front room and was frantically trying to get help even though he couldn't escape his loose ties. One reporter asked him about a previous conviction for assault and attempted rape but he waved off the question as not being relevant to the press conference. Except, it was.

Gordon was known to police in the area for a horrific attack he had carried out in the 1970s when he was only 17. He had attacked the wife of his school's science teacher with a knife and sexually assaulted her. The teacher went on to survive the attack and Gordon served four years in jail for the crime.

It was a worrying sign to the detectives that Gordon may have been involved in his own wife's murder but they had no real evidence to go on so they set up a crime scene reconstruction to have Gordon go over his story multiple times.

Holes in the story

On 2nd October, the police carried out a reconstruction of his movements, with Gordon alongside them. He retraced his steps of posting some letters in the early evening before going to The Brooklands pub on the outskirts of Coventry, having two drinks then driving home – where he found his wife being held at knifepoint.

The reconstruction was covered by local and national press, in the hopes that someone may come forward with more information but no one did, which was unusual, as Gordon had visited very public places but no one claimed to have seen him.

Staff and customers at The Brooklands had no recollection of Gordon drinking there that night, despite him being seen there on previous nights. There was also no evidence that suggested he had posted letters.

A day after the reconstruction, two Coventry-based sex workers went to police and said they recognised Gordon from numerous encounters between them, and that he preferred being tied up, along with 'kinky sex'. By that point, police were already suspicious of Gordon due to numerous reasons, not least his story.

The way that Gordon described his own attack didn't make sense. Gordon claimed that two men had come at him from both sides as he entered through the front door but there would not have been space for two men to be hiding.

Forensic experts found no trace of any chemical used to knock him out, nor was there any chemical delivered in that manner that could render a man unconscious in a few seconds and last for ten hours, despite Gordon claiming it to be a chloroform-based drug.

There was only one clown that night

It was odd for his clothes to be folded up and placed next to him after he had been tied up. It also remained odd for his clothes to have been removed in the first place and wasn't something that would have been required to tie him up.

His restraints were loose and it was concluded that anyone could have worked their wrists out of it. The fact that they were ratchet ties and not something like rope or cord, made it easier for a person to tie themselves up. The gag could easily have been put on before he tied himself. His bruises were also inconsistent with his story and were superficial.

And then there was The Woolwich. All branch managers, including Carol, were given special codes to use if they were being forced to unlock the branch or vault. The codes would unlock everything as normal but send a distress call to police. Carol hadn't used the distress codes.

With the holes in the story, police arrested Gordon on 20th October 1994 on the suspicion of his wife's murder. With no other suspects in the mix, he was charged four days later. His trial was held in 1995, with the prosecution claiming he had executed an elaborate scheme to deceive police, divert attention away from himself, and get away with murder.

The six week trial involved 128 witnesses, including numerous sex workers who identified Gordon as one of their clients. He was convicted of murder and robbery, and four days before Christmas in 1995, was sentenced to life in prison with a minimum tariff of 18 years.

An appeal was held in 2007, to reduce Gordon's sentence, but in the background, police had begun to link him to the murders of various sex workers around Coventry and Birmingham pre-1994 and fought to keep him in prison.

The judge at the appeal stated that Gordon would likely never be released and increased his life tariff to include an additional 18 years. Gordon still remains a suspect in the murders of at least two sex workers but has never been charged.

The murder of Carol Wardell and the resulting deception by Gordon is unlike any case seen in the area before or after. The only clown in the house that night was Gordon, who created the façade of a circus to ultimately get away with murder – which he didn't.

The House of Blood Murders

An argument between lovers resulted in a triple murder at a house in Glasgow, branded the House of Blood killings, with the ringleader known as the mother of all evil.

Until 2005, Glasgow, Scotland, was known as the murder capital of Europe, and not without warrant, the city had seen its fair share of horrific deaths. For a while, you were three times more likely to be murdered in Scotland than in England and Wales.

Scotland itself had the second highest European murder rate per capita, ranking close behind Finland, with both countries having a similar population level of 5.5million. To achieve the dishonourable title, Glasgow was witness to an average of 70 murders each year leading up to 2005.

By 2020-2021, murder in Glasgow had fallen by 50% and in that same statistic year had the lowest murder rate since 1976. Nowadays, it is improving, but at the tail end of its reign as Europe's murder capital, a bloody triple murder shocked the city and country.

It became known as the House of Blood killings, one of the bloodiest solved murders in Scotland in the 21st Century. The perpetrators used axes, knives, a hammer, golf clubs, a baseball bat, metal tools, lumps of wood, and a belt, to kill their victims.

And it all began after a lovers argument went wrong – very wrong.

Alcohol changes everything

In the autumn of 2004, 37-year-old Edith McAlinden was released from prison after serving a nine-month sentence for a serious assault. She had previously been convicted for robbery, was known to be a sex worker, and spent a lot of time homeless on the streets of Glasgow.

A few days after being released, on 16th October 2004, Edith went out drinking with her boyfriend,

42-year-old David Gillespie. By the time the evening came around, they had consumed a large amount of alcohol.

While out on the town, they met 67-year-old retired joiner Ian Mitchell, who they were both familiar with. After a few more drinks and getting friendly with them in the pub, Mitchell invited them back to his top floor flat in Crosshill.

Mitchell rented out one of the rooms in the flat to his friend, 71-year-old retired labourer Tony Coyle, who had gone out for the night. Coyle was born in the village of Bloody Foreland in Donegal, Ireland, and was a devout Catholic. Since retirement, he had spent his spare time carrying out repairs and gardening work for elderly neighbours and nearby residents.

Coyle was teetotal and hadn't drunk alcohol since he had retired, while Mitchell enjoyed the occasional drink. Gillespie on the other hand was known to drink heavily and was mostly spurred on by Edith, who always seemed to find a way to get drunk, despite not working.

On that fateful night in October, Edith and Gillespie were drinking heavily in Mitchell's flat when they began arguing with each other. Very quickly, the argument turned violent and Edith began hitting Gillespie.

Then out of nowhere, she grabbed a knife from the kitchen and stabbed him in the thigh. She had unknowingly severed a femoral vein in the leg which meant that Gillespie bled to death on the floor of Mitchell's apartment.

A family affair

Panicked by the thought of going back to prison, Edith refused to phone an ambulance, despite Mitchell begging her to. Instead, she made a phone call to her son, John, for help. Within minutes, 17-year-old John and his friend, 16-year-old Jamie Gray arrived in a taxi.

Edith begged Mitchell to pay for the taxi, which he did, without informing the taxi driver what had happened. Unbeknownst to Mitchell, Edith hadn't phoned her son for help, she had phoned him to help her eliminate any witnesses to the murder.

Understanding what was happening, John used a different knife and stabbed Mitchell before repeatedly kicking him in the head, causing his brain to bleed. They were wounds that ultimately killed him but they were not finished with him yet.

Shortly after midnight, Coyle returned home from visiting friends and saw that Mitchell's light was on. He popped his head around the door to wish him good night and saw the bloody carnage laid out in front of him.

He ran to his room and locked the door, barricading it with everything he could. Both John and Jamie tried to break the door down, before using drills to take it off the hinges. Once in the room, Jamie beat Coyle to death with a golf club.

But it didn't end there. To ensure the trio were dead, the killers used a wide variety of different weapons to bludgeon and beat their victims. In doing so, blood splattered the walls, sideboards, doors, kitchen units, hallway entrance, and floor.

They also boiled full kettles of water and poured them over Coyle's and Mitchell's heads to see if they were dead. They had killed all the witnesses but now needed to get away with it.

House of blood

Two hours later, at around 3am, without attempting to clean the crime scene, Edith went to a neighbour's house, the home of James Sweeney. She nervously claimed that something terrible had happened at Mitchell's flat and didn't know what to do.

Sweeney entered the flat, and only had to see the bloodied walls of the hallway to know that something horrific had gone down. Without realising there were three victims, he called the emergency services who arrived within minutes.

When police and paramedics arrived, they found Edith in the flat alone, hugging Gillespie's body. She was heard screaming at him to wake up and initially it was suspected the three dead were victims of gang violence, their bodies battered and beaten beyond recognition.

When reporters spoke to Sweeney, he told them of the blood-covered walls and floors, and they ran the story under the headline; *House of Blood*. As the morning hours brought with it a crisp breeze and grey skies, the truth of what happened was still unknown.

Police suggested that due to the amount of blood in the flat and the way it had been spread everywhere, there must have been at least two or three strong men involved. The same day, because of her lack of a cohesive story of what had gone down, Edith was charged with murder.

Mother of all evil

A large investigation began with police still sure that others had been involved. Edith claimed her innocence saying she had gone to the flat to meet her boyfriend and walked into the house of blood.

The investigation also hit an early difficulty, because due to the amount of blood splatter, it became difficult to ascertain the exact details of the violence. The medical examiner's office had on their hands not one, but three of the most brutal deaths they'd seen, and they had their work cut out.

The investigation suspected that Edith had not committed the murders alone and began a manhunt to snare the other culprits but they didn't have to wait long. The forensic team discovered evidence showing that both John and Jamie were involved.

They were arrested the following day and both charged with the murders but the police were not sure who had killed who. In the days that followed, the press got hold of the fact that Edith had called her son to help, which led to the headline; *Mother of all Evil*.

All three went to trial at Glasgow High Court in May 2005 and had initially pleaded not guilty. But as the trial went on, each of them confessed to one murder. Edith to killing Gillespie, John to killing Mitchell, and Jamie to killing Coyle.

Jurors were shown a police video of the murder scene and were warned that it was distressing. The flat had been trashed and covered with broken items and empty bottles of booze. There were also reported to be pieces of skull and brain stuck to the floor and curtains.

One month later, in a very public trial, Edith was convicted of murder and sentenced to life imprisonment with no eligibility for parole until 13 years later in 2018. John and Jamie were convicted of murder and sentenced to a minimum term of 12 years each.

Whereabouts unknown

The sentences were deemed to be too lenient by family members of the victims and they erupted in anger when the sentences were read out in court. A campaign was created to get the sentences extended but it ultimately went nowhere.

In early 2016, John was released a year early, but in November 2018 found himself back behind bars after threatening and abusing his girlfriend on a Glasgow street. His girlfriend refused to testify against him but John went back to jail for breaching the terms of his release.

Jamie was released early too but his whereabouts are unknown. Though he was 16 at the time, he was still considered an adult, and it is assumed he changed his identity to move on with a new life.

As for Edith, she initially had a tough time of it in prison, as fellow female prisoners were out for her blood, in revenge for the brutality of her crimes. She avoided being attacked by changing her demeanour and embarking on lesbian relationships with many other prisoners.

Details of her '*sex romps*' and prison violence were given to the press when one of her lovers was released from her sentence for drug dealing. It further cemented Edith's reputation as one of Glasgow's, and Scotland's, worst female criminals.

A search of the prison system showed that Edith had completed her sentence in 2018 and was released in 2019. Her whereabouts remain unknown and her identity hidden, most likely for her own protection.

Few in Crosshill or Glasgow will ever forget the brutality that Edith McAlinden inflicted on their city in 2004. Even under the unfortunate statistic of the murder capital of Europe, the House of Blood is a tale of triple murder that's hard to wash away.

Black Mass Poisoner

Black magic, witchcraft, poisonings, French aristocracy, hundreds of deaths, and a secret network of abortionists and fortune tellers, welcome to the tale of Catherine Monvoisin.

When it comes to body count, mystery, and utter bizarreness, the tale of Catherine Monvoisin will chill you to the white of your bones.

Born in 1640 France, 26 years after Elizabeth Bathory's demise at Castle Csejte, Catherine Monvoisin would become known across the city of Paris, and France, by her moniker of La Voisin. She plied her wares in the realm of fortune telling and was alleged to have been an advocate and practitioner of black magic.

Over time, she became the head of a large network of fortune tellers who provided macabre services to the French aristocracy and other wealthy people. These services included poisoning, abortion, arranging black masses, and the promotion and selling of dangerous aphrodisiacs.

Her crimes and those around her would eventually result in a major scandal in France that became known as the Affair of the Poisons during the reign of King Louis XIV. In the scandal, detailed in this tale, members of the aristocracy were charged with poisoning and witchcraft.

La Voisin became a central figure in the scandal due to her large network of evil fortune tellers. When details of the scandal were released over the passage of time, the public learned that La Voisin and her network had commissioned black magic rituals and poisonings said to have killed between 1,000 and 2,500 people.

When Catherine was a young woman, she married a jeweller and silk merchant named Antoine Monvoisin. Antoine's business went bust shortly after and he applied for bankruptcy. To support the family, Catherine, who was also a midwife at the time, turned to her one true passion to keep the bills paid.

Since the age of nine, she believed God had imbibed her with the power to heal others, through chiromancy and face-reading. From the early

1660s she turned to fortune telling as a way to bring in the money, but before she knew it, she was becoming one of the most popular fortune tellers in Paris.

As her spiritual abilities gained admiration across the region, she garnered the attention of some members of the French aristocracy and other wealthy people, who at the time believed in a fortune teller's ability to heal.

In 1664, she purchased an expensive crimson red velvet robe, said to have been embroidered with images of eagles in golden thread. As she developed her image as one of France's lead fortune tellers, she began to increase her client base rapidly.

From the mid-1660s, Catherine was supporting a family of six, including her children, her husband, and her mother. Though Antoine had become second-fiddle to his wife's illustrious career path. Catherine abused his position of trust and took at least six lovers while they were together.

Her lovers included an executioner, an alchemist, an architect, and a magician named Adam Lesage. Lesage was so besotted with Catherine, he attempted to coerce her into killing Antoine so he could have her all to himself. It is claimed she changed her mind at the last minute.

In 1665, a priest from the Saint Vincent de Paul's Order questioned Catherine's abilities in public, but not one to back down, she held a lecture in front of professors at Sorbonne University to explain how her gifts worked.

The professors were so convinced of her powers that they spread the word among their peers, and yet again, Catherine's clientele increased, to the point that she became a well-known figure in the King's court.

Important people began asking for advice and how to perform secret medical procedures, and it was then that things went a little bit more macabre. Enemies were beginning to rise on all sides, including many new fortune tellers, people wary of her powers, and some members of the aristocracy who believed what she was doing was tantamount to witchcraft.

Then, Catherine, now known as La Voisin, learned that many people who came to see her wished another person to be dead. Usually this had come out of a broken heart or straying lover, and the desired outcome was the death of a spouse or enemy.

La Voisin was also taking payments to carry out abortions in secret, which were illegal back then, as a side project to bring in more money for the family. It was this veil of secrecy surrounding her services that would lead to more people in power coming to her for help.

Realising she couldn't feed everyone's desires, she built a network of abortion providers who she could refer clients to on a referral fee basis. Which meant that when one member of her network was sent a client who wanted an abortion, La Voisin would keep a percentage of the fee – and get richer.

It was claimed the underground abortion industry was so large in 17th Century France, that many of the foetuses were burned in a furnace and buried in La Voisin's garden. Though when it came to the trial, the abortion side of the story took a back seat to the poisonings.

To capitalise on people's desire to heal, kill, and tread between the line of right and wrong, she expanded her services to include the selling of potions and powders. On top of her fortune telling, she began to sell poisons to her clients.

Some of the potions contained the bones of toads, powdered teeth, iron dust, human blood, human ashes, and an aphrodisiac known as Lytta Vesicatoria, or more commonly; Spanish Fly.

She would put her clients through a gradual program of church visits to praise a particular saint, and when that didn't work, which it undoubtedly didn't, then she would move onto amulets, magic objects, and then ultimately the poisons.

By this point she was known to be performing black masses, in which she used a woman's body as a living altar for spirits to be worshipped. For a large fee, she allowed her client to pray to Satan for their wishes or desires to be made true.

On those occasions, she would arrange for a woman to be laid or sat at an altar. There, she would place a bowl on the woman, hold a baby above the bowl, and sacrifice the baby so that its blood could flow freely into the bowl. It is suspected the babies were stillborn or had already died from natural causes, rather than being alive.

Poisoning in the 17th Century was an art form, a novelty to come out of the alchemist's lab. Just two decades before La Voisin, an Italian poisoner named Giulia Tofana had perfected the art of combining various ingredients. Yet, La Voisin was the one to perfect it for criminal purposes.

As her abortion network grew in size, La Voisin realised she could supply her poisons to the same network alongside a newly developed network of fortune tellers she had been overseeing. So, as the clients grew, more and more poisonings were taking place – and people were dying across the city.

In 1667, La Voison received a visit from Claude de Vin des Oeillets, who was a companion and confidant to Madame de Montespan, a mistress of King Louis XIV. Having heard of La Voisin's incredible powers, Montespan recruited her to help win the love of King Louis.

At a large mansion, on the ancient streets of Paris, La Voison and other magicians held a secret black mass for Montespan while she prayed to win the love of the King. The same year, Montespan became the official mistress of the King and put her good fortune down to La Voison.

Montespan then sought La Voison's special skills whenever a problem occurred both in her personal and professional life. This solidified La Voison's position among the French aristocracy for the next six years.

In 1673, Montespan was suspicious the King was cheating on her with another mistress and employed the services of La Voison to perform multiple black masses. At least one of the black masses involved Montespan as the female altar herself.

An engraving in 1895 by Henry de Malvost shows a nude Montespan on the altar having a baby's blood splashed on to her, with La Voison standing nearby. La Voisin provided aphrodisiacs to Montespan so she could poison the King with it.

In 1679, the King fell into a relationship with Angélique de Fontanges. Enraged, Montespan begged La Voison to kill King Louis, and she eventually agreed. La Voison recruited some of her own closest confidants and they came up with a plan.

They decided to poison a petition which would be delivered to the King himself and placed into his hands where the poison would be absorbed by his skin.

In March of 1679, La Voison went to the royal court to deliver the petition but failed to get it past the other petitioners. She returned home and had it burned then tried to work out another plan to kill the King.

But her past was catching up to her and rumours of a secret network of witches and poisoners were already rampant among the French public. Just three years earlier, the King's sister-in-law, Duchesse d'Orléans, was suspected to have been poisoned to death.

At her funeral, a riot had taken place where the public were accusing witches of abducting their children for sacrifice in black masses. At the same time, priests and churches were warning the royal court and police that a huge number of people were confessing to poisoning others.

A day after visiting the royal court, La Voison was arrested outside of Notre Dame after a meeting to decide how to kill the King. Hearing about the secret network of poisoners, King Louis issued an order to exterminate the network throughout the city and country.

Up until December 1679, many involved in La Voison's network were arrested, including her own daughter, and the magicians involved in the black masses. The King issued another order giving permission for the use of torture to interrogate the prisoners.

Other high-ranking officials of the aristocracy hushed the order to torture La Voison in case she revealed too many names of people involved. Yet, La Voison knew she had been caught and eventually confessed to having sold poison and black magic services to people within the royal court.

La Voison was found guilty of witchcraft and sentenced to death by burning. Despite being tortured from her sentencing to execution, she refused to name the people within the Royal Court.

On 22nd February 1680, La Voison was strapped to the stake and burned alive.

In July 1680, La Voison's daughter confessed there was a plan in place to poison the King, which had been arranged by people close to the King, including Montespan. The King was outraged that members of the royal court were involved. He closed the investigation and shut down the court where the trials were taking place.

The King signed a royal order known as a '*lettre de cachet*' which was an order to enforce a judgement that could not be appealed. It fundamentally removed all of the suspects and prisoners involved in the poisoning case out of the public judicial system and into secrecy.

Many, including La Voison's daughter, were secretly sentenced to perpetual imprisonment in fortresses around the country until their deaths. The commanders of the fortresses were ordered to torture them if they were about to reveal the names of people involved.

Montespan was not publicly disgraced and retired somewhat gracefully to the Filles de Saint-Joseph convent, in the rue Saint-Dominique. Thankful for her departure, the King made her father the governor of Paris. Little justice it seemed for the woman who wanted the King dead.

Other suspects and prisoners escaped the King's order due to the power they still wielded among their peers. Some were banished from Paris and others fled into exile.

The court set up to put witches on trial was abandoned by the King in 1682, as he couldn't risk a public scandal. Over the course of the Affairs of the Poisons, 218 suspects had been arrested, with another 200 unidentified. Out of those, 36 were executed for poisoning or witchcraft. Details of the trial were eventually released as the passage of time went by.

In a book called *Sex with Kings*, by Eleanor Herman, it is claimed police uncovered the remains of 2,500 infants in La Voisin's garden. The size of La Voison's poison network was alleged to have killed at least 1,000 people. Reports from priests and other statements at the time seem to imply this was a conservative figure. La Voison will forever be connected with the reign of King Louis XIV, in a moment of history that still defies belief to this day.

Killer In the Walls

A creepy intruder terrorised a family by living in the walls of their home and making them think the house was haunted, in a true urban legend that ended with multiple murder.

Many horror stories flip the notion that a home should be safe and protected and turn it into a place of nightmarish terror and fear. Horror turns home security on its head by giving us haunted houses, poltergeists, home invasions, and secrets in the basement.

Like many great stories, most are based on some elements of truth, and none more so than the killer who hid in the walls of a family home and made them believe it was haunted. Giving us a haunted house and invasion tale in one.

In Townsend, Massachusetts, in 1986, 16-year-old schoolgirl Annie Andrews was excited to be going on a blind date with a guy she had spoken to on the phone. Her life had been going downhill, with her mother dying of cancer just a few months earlier.

She lived with her father, Brian, and younger sister, Jessica, in a large house on the far side of town. Out of the blue, Annie received a phone call from a teenage boy named Daniel LaPlante. He said he got her number from some friends and that they went to the same school together.

Daniel described himself as tall, blond, athletic, and handsome, and lived close by. Taken by his charm, Annie agreed to go on a date with him, except, when they met, Daniel wasn't quite what he claimed to be.

Forged in violence and abuse

She had made the mistake of inviting him over to her house, but when she opened the door, she saw that Daniel had greasy black hair and was wearing dirty clothes. He wasn't athletic, and Annie agreed with herself that he wasn't handsome. Still, she decided to go on the date with him.

They went into town and had some ice cream from a local café, which was the best part of the date, because everything else was horrible. Daniel was insistent that Annie talked to him about her recently dead mother and began asking inappropriate questions about her sexuality.

Annie quickly ended the date and refused to answer any more phone calls from him, but she was a little fearful that Daniel knew where she lived. Unknown to Annie, Daniel wasn't quite finished with her.

Daniel was born in 1970 to a violent father who beat and sexually abused him throughout his formative years. It was later confirmed that Daniel had also been abused by many family friends around the same time.

Unsurprisingly, the abuse affected every aspect of his life and he struggled academically and socially. He had no friends, was an outcast at school, and was often described as the weird one. The school sent him to a psychiatrist who diagnosed him with multiple disorders.

It was with unfortunate hindsight that the psychiatrist would also abuse Daniel and make him perform sexual acts. It seemed wherever Daniel went, he was losing his grip on humanity. Until he became infatuated with Annie.

The haunting

Due to the recent loss of their mother, Annie and Jessica decided to hold a séance in the basement of their home. They wanted to try and reach out to their mother and tell her how much they loved her. Although nothing strange happened during the séance, what happened after was freaky.

That same night, while in their beds, both girls heard a mysterious knocking and concluded they had invoked an evil spirit. They asked questions to the spirit and were shocked when it answered by tapping on the walls. But it didn't end there.

The knocking on the walls continued at all hours of the day and night and was beginning to freak the sisters out. They told their father, Brian, who laughed it off and said they were making it all up, and that they should never mess with the ways of the occult.

In the days and weeks that followed the séance, more strange things started happening. Sometimes, the furniture had been moved into different positions, and items from the kitchen were found in different parts of the house.

Items they placed on the dining table were later found on the floor beside the table, displayed in an unusual manner. The knocking also continued in various parts of the house, and also when the girls would shower.

They also found written signs on mirrors, and their undergarments moved from drawer to drawer.

Still, Brian didn't believe them and put it down to the loss of their mother affecting them. Then, after finding a note in their bedroom that read, *'I'm back, find me if you can,'* and words written in blood on the basement wall, the sisters ran screaming from the house.

Descent into murder

While at work, Brian received word from his neighbours that his daughters were with them. He returned home to find the words in the basement had been written with ketchup and not blood. When he went upstairs to the bedroom, he found Daniel, dressed up in the clothes of his deceased wife.

They got into a fight but Daniel managed to escape and disappear, seemingly into thin air. When police searched the house, they found a hidden section behind Annie's closet. When they went inside, they found Daniel hiding in the walls of the house.

An investigation discovered that Daniel had been hiding in the walls and crawlspace of the house for many weeks and had made peepholes into the walls to spy on the family, even in the bathroom, and the girl's bedrooms.

Daniel was only sentenced to a few months in juvenile detention for trespassing and inciting fear.

He was out on the streets within a couple of months and began stealing from shops and houses. On one of his raids, he stole two guns.

On 1st December 1987, during the day, he broke into the Gustafson household, only a mile from Annie's house. He stumbled across 33-year-old pregnant mother Priscilla Gustafson and her two children, seven-year-old Abigail and five-year-old William.

Daniel raped Priscilla in front of her children then shot her at point blank range in the head. He then strangled Abigail, hit her over the head, and drowned her face-down in the downstairs bathtub. He drowned William in the upstairs bathtub.

Andrew Gustafson returned home at 5pm and discovered his family had been slaughtered, including his unborn baby.

Urban legend

It didn't take long for investigators to link Daniel to the murders. There was a lot of genetic evidence left at the crime scene, and many of the stolen items were found in a search of Daniel's family home. He was arrested and quickly sent to trial.

In 1988, 18-year-old Daniel was sentenced to three consecutive life sentences for the murders of the

Gustafson family. There was no death penalty in Massachusetts at the time, and life without parole was the maximum penalty available.

In 2013, Daniel allegedly became a Wiccan and tried to sue the state of Massachusetts for not allowing him access to various items to practice the modern Pagan religion. He failed. In a 2017 parole hearing, he was resentenced due to a psychiatrist's report that stated Daniel showed no remorse.

A 2019 parole hearing, held due to a change in sentences relating to crimes committed by minors, upheld the sentences, meaning that Daniel is unlikely to ever be released into the community.

His crimes as a teenager are as horrific as they are creepy, forged in the hell of child abuse, he inflicted that pain upon others. The next time you hear knocking on the walls, it might not be that ghostly spirit you invoked, but the creepy urban legend of someone living in the walls of your home.

The Ughill Hall Murders

In a double murder that shocked Sheffield, a successful solicitor killed his mistress and her daughter, and left her son for dead, before fleeing to France and threatening to jump off the Amiens Cathedral.

With an urban population of 730,000 (2020), Sheffield is one of the largest cities in the UK and played a big part historically in the Industrial Revolution from 1760 to 1840. It also has a long sporting history and is home to Sandygate; the world's oldest football ground, first opened in 1804.

History plays a big part in the city and so it's no surprise that crime has also left its mark. Now considered a relatively safe city, Sheffield has been home to some of the most notorious murders in middle England, including The East House Murders and The Blonk Street Murder.

But there is one incident from the 1980s that seemed to have a bigger effect on locals, with many claiming to have links to the family involved, and the survivor of the attack. It forever tainted the quaint village of Ughill, on the outskirts of the city.

On 21st September 1986, solicitor Ian Wood shot dead his French mistress, Danielle Ledez, her three-year-old daughter Stephanie, and left her five-year-old son Christopher for dead, after shooting him twice in the head.

He fled to France and went on the run before climbing the Cathedral Basilica of Our Lady of Amiens, also known as the Amiens Cathedral, in the Picardy region of the country, and threatening to jump to his death in front of a large crowd.

Splashing the cash

The whole sordid affair began a few years earlier when Wood left his wife of a number of years and his three children to hook up with his French mistress, Danielle. Wood, born in 1949, was a successful solicitor, and the fruits of his labour were large.

So large in fact, that in 1986 at the age of 37, he was able to rent an 18-bedroom mansion called Ughill Hall. Within the confines of Sheffield, he had set up his own legal practice with many employees and had become chairman of the Sheffield Law Society.

Known as a bit of a playboy, he was open to splashing the cash while out and about, regularly hosted dinner parties for some of Sheffield's finest, and was known to buy lavish gifts for others, either to keep them close or as a display of wealth.

He began renting Ughill Hall in April 1986 and moved in with Danielle and her two children. Danielle was a French teacher from Amiens, who was living in England when she met Wood.

She was in the process of divorcing her second husband when she moved into Ughill Hall, and was already 10 weeks pregnant, allegedly with Wood's child, though the unborn child's parentage was never proven.

Gun collector turned murderer

Wood was a gun collector, who had inherited a .38 Enfield revolver from his father after he took his own life with it. The gun was the standard British sidearm used during the Second World War and was manufactured between 1930 and 1957.

His father's suicide left an indelible mark on Wood's life and was something he would later use in his defence at the trial. By 1985, Wood had amassed a collection of 10 guns that were stored at his home, where he lived with his first wife.

In December 1985, when he turned to alcohol because of existing mental health conditions, including depression, his wife had the collection officially confiscated. The collection was returned to Wood two weeks later as South Yorkshire Police couldn't find any evidence to suggest he was a threat to himself or others, despite being diagnosed with depression.

A few weeks after that, the guns were confiscated again due to an administrative mix-up with his firearm license. They were returned a second time in February 1986. A month later in March, Wood purchased 50 rounds of ammunition for his father's revolver.

On the night of 21st September 1986, and for reasons then unknown, Wood, then 37, decided to kill his new family. At around midnight, he went to the playroom of the mansion where Danielle was resting and murdered her with a bullet to the head.

He then took three-year-old Stephanie from her bedroom and asked her to play hide and seek. She sleepily agreed and he led her to Christopher's bedroom, where he shot her twice in the back of the head, killing her instantly. Five-year-old Christopher was removed from his bedroom and taken to one of the bathrooms.

Wood told him to close his eyes as he had a surprise for him. When Christopher put his hands over his eyes, Wood shot him twice in the head at point blank range, then used a large metal ruler to beat him before leaving his body with the others in the playroom. Remarkably, Christopher would go on to survive the attack.

Miracle survivor

Wood then calmly began the process of leaving the mansion. He packed a suitcase, changed his clothes, and left the property in the early hours of the morning. He left the revolver on the kitchen worktop, with one live round inside.

He drove to Dover in a rented car and caught a ferry to France later that morning. Shortly before he boarded, he phoned the police and told them he had murdered Danielle and her family. On the evening of the 22nd, police arrived at the mansion.

All the doors and windows were locked, and with no answer, they smashed down the front door. Due to the size of the mansion, they didn't find the bodies immediately, but when they entered the playroom, they walked in on a grizzly sight.

The two children had been laid next to their mother in a pool of blood. It was clear to police they had all been shot, but when one officer checked Christopher's body for signs of life, he was shocked to discover the boy was alive.

After 21 hours of laying on the floor next to his family members, Christopher was rushed to Royal Hallamshire Hospital for children where doctors fought to save his life. Two bullets were removed from his head, and he was placed on life support.

On the run

Believing Wood to still be in and around Sheffield, police put his wife and three children under police protection and warned the public not to approach him as he may have been in possession of a firearm. Four additional families were placed under police protection in relation to the case.

Two days after the murders, on the 23rd, Wood phoned a reporter called Brenda Tunny who worked for the local Sheffield Weekly Gazette. She interrupted a police press conference to inform them of the contact she'd had.

During the phone call, Wood had asked about funeral arrangements and told her how he killed the family. Over the next few days, he phoned Brenda another eight times. Over the course of the phone calls, he spoke about taking his own life, and claimed he killed Danielle due to a suicide pact but refused to give his location.

Shortly after the first phone call, an AA (Automobile Association) admin clerk contacted police and told them Wood had applied for an international driving license. Interpol were called in, and the investigation linked up with French authorities.

On 29th September, eight days after the murders, and with international attention focused on the case, Wood travelled to Amiens where he joined a public tour of Amiens Cathedral. The famous building was only three miles from where Danielle had been born.

He left the tour group and climbed to the top of the cathedral where he stepped over the top wall and roped himself to a gargoyle. The intention was to jump off the gargoyle to hang himself, 61-metres (200ft) from the hard ground below.

The authorities arrived quickly after receiving multiple reports and discovered that Wood had left a suicide note with a member of staff. He remained roped to the gargoyle for almost seven hours until a local priest, assisted by the police, talked him down.

Suicide pact

Wood was taken into custody and claimed that when he saw the amount of people gathered on the ground watching him, he couldn't jump as he didn't want an audience for his death. After a lengthy extradition process, Wood was flown back to the UK on 19th November to face trial.

The trial began in early February 1987 and Wood was charged with two counts of murder and one of attempted murder. He pleaded guilty to Stephanie's murder and Christopher's attempted murder but pleaded not guilty to Danielle's murder.

He claimed that it was manslaughter and not murder, because they had agreed to a suicide pact. In the UK at the time, there was a law that stated if a person killed another person on the basis of a suicide pact and didn't take their own life after, then they would be guilty of manslaughter and not murder – but they needed to prove there was a pact in place.

Wood's defence put forward his five step suicide pact. Wood was to kill the family then visit a

French church to light candles for them. Then phone the press and explain what had happened, kill Danielle's husband, ensure they were all buried in France, then visit their graves and lay flowers for them.

The unusual five step pact was not believed and Wood was found guilty of two murders and one attempted murder. In July 1987, Wood was sentenced to life imprisonment for each murder and an additional 12 years for attempted murder.

After the trial, the police were scrutinised for allowing Wood to have access to so many weapons. Wood's doctor had advised the police to confiscate the weapons just weeks before the murders, on the basis that Wood appeared mentally distressed.

Life finds a way

Less than a month later, on 19th August, 27-year-old Michael Ryan shot dead 16 people in Berkshire, in an event that became known as the Hungerford Massacre. Both events saw the government pass the Firearms Act 1988 which banned ownership of semi-automatic weapons and required psychiatric assessments to be completed.

The courthouse where the trial took place was abandoned in 1997 and left to rot, becoming a popular site for urban explorers. In 2019, plans had been submitted by new owners to turn it into a hotel but failed when they ran into financial trouble. The giant building went to auction in 2021 at a guide price of only £750,000 but got no bidders. It remains abandoned.

Wood's whereabouts are unknown but he was suspected to have been moved to a locked psychiatric facility, and as such, is difficult to track. If he had been released, it would have happened quietly and under a new name.

Christopher Ledez made a recovery but was physically and mentally scarred by the shootings. He has never publicly spoken about what happened but is known to have moved on with his life, is now married, and has children of his own, proving that life will always find a way.

As a thank you for adding this book to your collection, we would like to offer you a FREE eBook for simply signing up to our mailing list. Along with a free book, you'll get weekly updates from the world of true crime brought to you by truecrimelists.com, and early book release notifications so you can be the first to get them at an introductory price, exclusively for subscribers.

Visit WWW.TRUECRIMELISTS.COM and click on FREE BOOK from the menu.

www.ingramcontent.com/pod-product-compliance
Lightning Source LLC
LaVergne TN
LVHW051116080426
835510LV00018B/2061